The Connection

Connection List ➤	➤ Wave of Connectivity
Employee Engagement ➤	➤ Success
Delegation ➤	➤ Accountability
Success Planning, Talent Development ➤	➤ Exit Strategy
Data, Metrics, Analyses ➤	➤ ROI Growth
Strategic Alliances ➤	➤ Networking
Research-Self ➤	➤ Research-Competitors
60 Seconds to Connect ➤	➤ Start with the End in Mind
Business Plan ➤	➤ Branding
Desire ➤	➤ Achievement

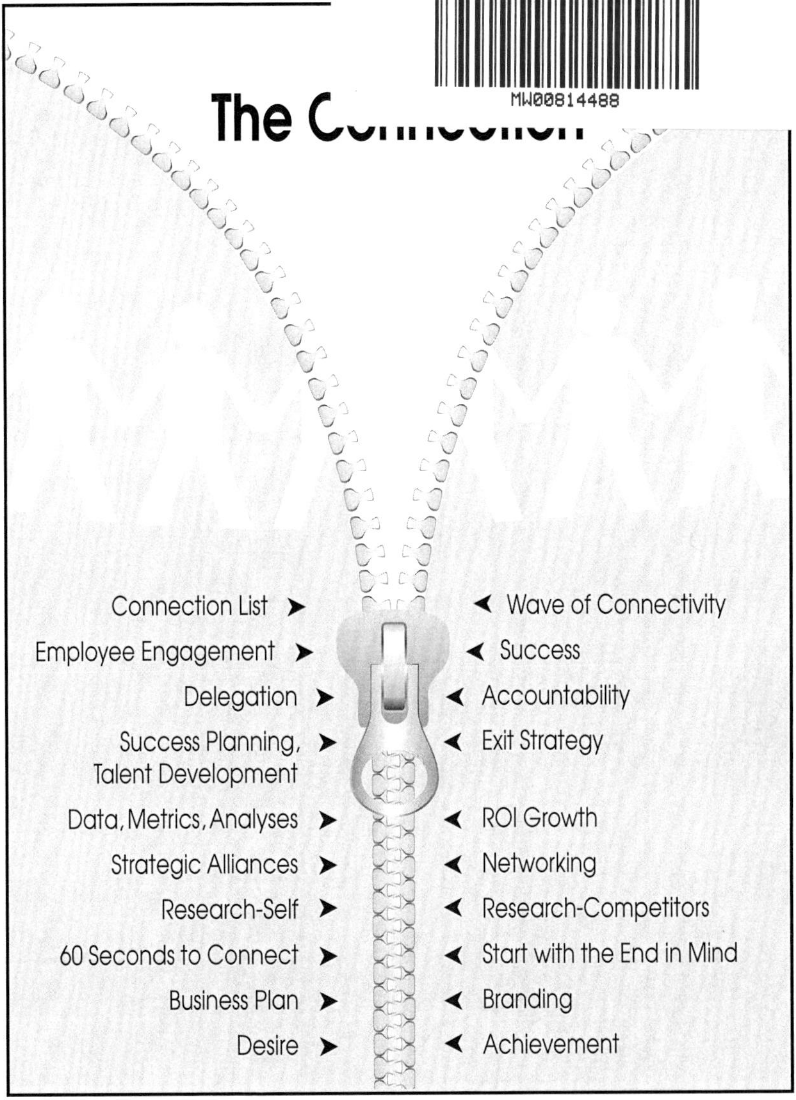

Printed by Apollo Press, Inc.

ISBN 978-0-692-23557-7

Printed in the Unites States of America.

The Connection

THE PLAYBOOK FOR
BUSINESS OWNERS & EXECUTIVES

LEARN HOW TO MAKE
ALL OF YOUR CONNECTIONS COUNT +
THE ONES YOU HAVEN'T CONNECTED TO YET

ACKNOWLEDGEMENTS

This book has been a labor of love with an enormous amount of support from my family, friends, colleagues, clients and strategic alliances. I'm so grateful for:

My amazing husband, Keith, and all of his ongoing support while writing this book and throughout life. My three wonderful children that keep me going, focused and who make life and connecting worth doing to begin with: Davis, Serena, and Tony. My mother, Elaine, who has made me the person I am today and hope to be tomorrow. Her strength is, simply put, generous to say the least. My sister, Angel, for her support and feedback.

...contributors with the book including input, directing and creative design. Dr. Chris Neck (influencing, supporting, motivating, believing, connecting, kindness), Elizabeth Veliz, Adelante HR Solutions, LLC (Chapter 9 contributor, strong strategic partner and friend), Melinda Evans, Designs by ME (amazing graphic illustrator and book designer), InnerCirque, a Creative Consortium (editing), Kathy Taylor (Apollo Press) and Colin Taylor, Purpose in Profits (motivating, supporting, coaching, inspiring) – I thank each of you.

...clients over the years that help mold the connecting abilities, stories, and allowing me to be a part of their lives and their companies: Ken Kovach, Kathy Howell, Oscar Alvarez, Fadwa Hasan, Teresa Robinson, and so many more.

...friends and connections made over the years that have given me ideas and support sometimes without even knowing it: Jennifer Morrone, Dan Pink, Cathy Lanier, Sarah Miller Caldicott, Lynn Spencer, Liz Wizeman, Eleanor Clift, Perry Hooks, Loretta Yenson, Jim White and all the women in the Peninsula Women's Network as well as all of my fellow Predictive Index consultants at PI Midlantic. I so appreciate our interactions and time together.

TABLE OF CONTENTS

FOREWORD

Christopher P. Neck
University Master Teacher
Associate Professor of Management
Arizona State University
www.chrisneck.com

Steven Jobs once remarked:

"Creativity is just connecting things. When you ask creative people how they did something, they feel a little guilty because they didn't really do it, they just saw something. It seemed obvious to them after a while. That's because they were able to connect experiences they've had and synthesize new things."

With this quotation in mind and with all due respect to Mr. Jobs, I feel that he undersold the value of "connecting." The power of connection goes far beyond better creativity.

Shelley Smith's *THE CONNECTION* builds upon this premise as she shows you how "connecting" yourself and your business with opportunities can lead to not only more creativity but also improved success in your personal and professional life.

While there are other books that talk about connecting with events and people and the importance of it, Shelley Smith's book stands out because she tells you not only the "why" of connecting but also the "how." Read this book and you will be able to better connect with the opportunities that exist in your world.

In fact, when I think of "connecting" I think of Shelley Smith. She is the connection expert in my opinion and her expertise shines through in this book. In the movie, *The Shawshank Redemption*, the character, "Red" (played by Morgan Freeman) was the prisoner that everyone went to when they needed something (whether it was gum or a poster). Red had power in the prison because he was able to connect people with things they needed. Shelley Smith is "Red" in real life. I personally go to her when I need something (such as a guest speaker for a class, or a story for a speech) because I know she is the master at connecting people with what they need.

Shelley combines her real-life "connecting" experiences with scholarly knowledge as she presents chapter after chapter on connection-related topics to help you better grasp the opportunities that exist in your sphere right now.

In conclusion, this is a book that will teach you about connecting, make you think, and hopefully move you to reach out and seize the opportunities that confront you now and into the future. It takes a talented writer to do all of these things

and Shelley does just that! So enjoy Shelley's journey as you read through the pages of *THE CONNECTION*.

May 27, 2014

INTRODUCTION

This book is about truly making "**The Connection**". I have a strong belief that once you really understand the importance of **connecting**, only then can you truly break through. It's time to live and be clear about your own success and sense of purpose, all the while creating success for those with and around you.

To fully understand, follow and embrace the intentions of this book, you have to be open to the definitions and vast opportunities in the word "**connection.**"

- *How do you* ***connect*** *your desire to your achievements? How do you achieve more by* ***connecting*** *and interacting with others?*

- *How can research help you* ***connect*** *to your company's potential growth? How can research* ***connect*** *the missing pieces to your true billable rate and ROI or that of your company? Did you know mapping your revenue streams back to your* ***connections and*** *provides you with a clear picture of what does and doesn't work with your overall business development?*

- *Do you know how the right executive coach can help you* ***connect*** *and tap into your knowledge, skills and passions to become laser-focused, therefore more productive?*

- *Do you know how to utilize your* ***connections*** *when you already feel at the top of your game and unclear what you can do next? Can you make the* ***connections*** *and use your knowledge to keep you challenged and on a continual trajectory of self-defined success?*

- *Do you know the* ***connection*** *between training, development, succession planning, replacement planning and the best avenues to take for each and when?*

- *Do you understand the ROI you receive when* ***connecting*** *those in your organization to the right kind of training and overall wellness?*

These questions and many more are answered in this "how-to Playbook," ***The Connection***. Discover topics you have never been shown or heard about as well as revisit some well-known basics but written with a "call to action" viewpoint.

My intentions began with a strong desire to teach, share, motivate, inspire and **connect** others in the direction their passions and God-given talents can take them. When we learn something, we should share it, it's just that plain and simple to me. That is a **CONNECTION!**

I have had the pleasure in life of enjoying my career choices. Yes, they have been tough at times but I have generally always liked, and more often than not "loved," the job I wake up to every day, the job I connected to. I know that may be hard to believe but I was raised to follow my dreams, my heart and most definitely my passions. It probably doesn't hurt to always believe the glass is half to three-quarters full.

Learning something and **connecting** the pieces out of every perceivably bad situation is another must, keeping in mind that experience comes when something didn't go the way you originally envisioned it. **Connecting** what happened with how to pivot makes putting the next round of goal-reaching tactics into action much easier.

So again, why this book? I am a generalist and have had the pleasure and honor of being exposed to, and **connected** with, many experts in their fields over the past 35 years. This book tells some of their stories, highlights some of my favorite connection-making reading materials and provides you with tips, how tos, calls to action. Along the way you'll discover the reasoning behind my calling this a Playbook that illustrates the many ways you can **connect.**

You can read from the beginning to the end, or you can skip around. The book provides examples for the sole proprietors, entrepreneurs, freelancers and, of course, large business owners and senior executives.

The opening chapter starts with the necessity for a strong desire to achieve, to learn, to be the best you can be. Desire comes when you WANT to do something vs. HAVE to do something. I have always worked long hours in the corporate world, and now with my own business. But for the most part, that has always been by choice, a choice driven by desire. **Connecting** your desires to your achievements is a great place for us to start.

So…enjoy the book, the specifics, the tips, the ideas. Share with others, don't hold onto what you have learned; share it and watch it multiply. It's the best feeling in the world AND it works in every walk of life!

Let's get started and make some C**ONNECTIONS**!

MAKING THE CONNECTION BETWEEN DESIRE AND ACHIEVEMENT

"Do stuff. Be clenched, curious. Not waiting for inspiration's shove or society's kiss on your forehead. Pay attention. It's all about paying attention, attention is vitality. It connects you with others. It makes you eager, stay eager."

Susan Sontag

CHAPTER 1

Desire is a funny thing that can be perceived in different ways. Keeping that in mind, how you react to and pursue your desires will vary based on your level of knowledge, persistence to act, and ultimately, connect.

Defining **Desire** as:

1) To long or hope for: exhibit or feel desire for.
2) To express a wish for.

<u>Defining **Achievement** as:</u>

1) A thing done successfully, typically by effort, courage, or skill.
2) The process or fact of achieving something.

<u>Defining **Connection** as:</u>

1) A relationship in which a person, thing, or idea is linked or associated with something else.

When we make the connection between the longing for something and successfully attaining that goal, the more satisfying the achievement becomes, carrying the potential for a ripple effect. When your achievement stems from a strong desire, you naturally feel you've accomplished even more and thus the achievement ripple is more powerful and rewarding.

<u>Making the Full Connection</u>

Step 1

Desire + Drive = Satisfaction in Achievement

One of my clients—let's call her Desiree—had a thriving design firm. By all accounts she was very successful. She measured her success based on her goals of clothing designs in production and her continued need to add staffing.

Desiree thought she was ready for the "big move"–opening a storefront retail shop. At least, everyone had convinced her it was the right next move, one that would validate her and position her for continued growth.

Desiree approached me to help her through the entire process. As we examined her books to put together her business plan for the bank, I began to see not only her passion in the design and personal touch she put into each clothing line but also the importance of work-life balance. Desiree thought that the next step meant she had to have a warehouse as well as a storefront location. She hadn't considered the idea of using an online outlet to keep her overhead down and profit margins up. Upon further investigation, I saw that while Desiree had grown over the past years in top line revenue, her margins continued to decrease and the hours she worked increased. Again, she thought she just needed to make that big move. But this was a step that would take her from running in the "green" to running and living in the "red" until the sales volume at the retail store was enough to offset all her new-found overhead. To get straight to the point, Desiree was connected to the creative side of the business and to the personal relationships she had established with her clients over the past 10 years. She really had no desire to go big and go retail. She preferred to remain a niche designer with work-life balance, who had greater profit margins with smaller volume. Once she realized that it was okay to remain passionate, creative and personal-relationship focused, she was able to put aside the "need" for a retail store. Once the desire/achievement dynamic was identified, the pressure was off and she was able to once again focus and successfully continue to grow her business month after month as well as her profit margins–while keeping the hours and lifestyle she desired. We are now looking at succession planning and the next steps to keep her financial future intact and fruitful. Desiree received her "hall pass" in life once she shed her false perceptions. She came back to her passions and therefore achieved more, once she made the connection and focus. She is still riding those ripples of success and achievement today. *In a future chapter you will hear how to break down revenue segments to get at the most profitable sides of your business and your personal hourly rate.*

MAKING YOUR OWN CONNECTIONS

This opening chapter is a call to connect your desires, your passions, your skills and your talents and link them to other people, other things, processes, systems, results and greater productivity.

If you don't first desire, then you will not move forward and therefore will not make the connections and achieve what you are pursuing. Our pursuit of happiness is more readily fulfilled by the desire to move forward, and preferably move forward with those things we are truly passionate about in life with focus on our God-given talents and strengths.

The stronger our drive, the more focused and aggressive the pursuit of our passions. For some, drive and

desire are not enough. "We don't know what we don't know," or even how to move forward. In the next chapters you will find suggestions and processes to move towards continued development of self both professionally and personally. These chapters can be applied to many walks of life personally and professionally. Staying fully connected, and having the right people supporting you, will help you continue the journey.

We can achieve more in the process when we work with, engage and collaborate with others through all the natural connections. Self-accountability and awareness will become clearer with these processes as we break them down and make it more comfortable to ask for help from others instead of perhaps feeling defeated when asking or feeling under-accomplished.

Opening yourself up to conversations with those you respect and trust can be the breakthrough you need. When we share with others, we get immediate feedback emotionally, verbally and through reactions in body language. Those reactions can further confirm what we thought to be true or help us pivot and adjust as needed.

More often than not, we need to pivot and that's okay. Taking in other perspectives helps you to become laser sharp with your area of focus. Take a moment and think about those in your life, your inner circle, people who can give you the feedback, the insight, the clarity you need. Those could include your immediate family members, your peers, your colleagues, your immediate supervisor, your church family, those in your networking group or even a childhood friend who knows you best.

Who knows what you can achieve, what your company and your team can achieve, when you react on your desires to move forward, to push the elements of your business and life to full connect and be fully engaged? When you do this well, you take your entourage with you directly and indirectly. There is a great book I reference all the time with clients called *Multipliers* by Liz Wiseman, *How the Best Leaders make Everyone Smarter*. Her focus and message are right on target with everything I believe to be true. A great leader, an inspirational leader, a successful leader is one who lifts you up, increases your mojo, helps you with the "what ifs" in life and pushes you to embrace challenges and move forward—most certainly to "be all you can be."

ARE YOU MISSING THE CONNECTION DUE TO ROAD BLOCKS AND EXCUSES?

Here are some common roadblocks and/or myths that can stop us along the way to achieving our goals. Have you heard of these or thought of them yourself?

- I am already at the top of my game.
- I don't have funds or it's not in the budget.
- My talents don't match my career of choice.
- This is what the members in my family have always done.

- This is how the company /department has always been run.
- We are already increasing our profit annually.
- I don't see a need for change or pivoting.
- I don't have the energy to pursue my thoughts and desires.
- I don't have the support of my family.
- I don't have the right staff.
- I don't have time.
- I am retiring soon.
- The company's culture doesn't allow for this type of development.
- It's not my responsibility to be a multiplier.
- My boss doesn't motivate me, so why should I try and motivate those around me?
- It's not my agenda, it's my supervisor's.

Some of these statements can be "hard stoppers" if you are already putting limitations on yourself and haven't even begun to ask the question "what if," which can lead to your desire to change, achieve and move forward, critical steps that ultimately allow you to make *The Connection.*

ACTION IS CALLING: REVIEW THE PLAYBOOK AND THE DESIRE TO CONNECT

So…what are you waiting for? What have you put on your list but haven't accomplished and/or pursued? Why? What's holding you back? Please stop and make a list or write a statement in this book, or your journal or on a sticky note, so you can go back while reading this book and take a look, stop, reflect and adjust to move forward, keeping in mind you may need to pivot along the way.

Desires & Making the Connection Accountability List	
Desires and Passions	The excuses that are holding you back or the misconceptions you are holding onto.

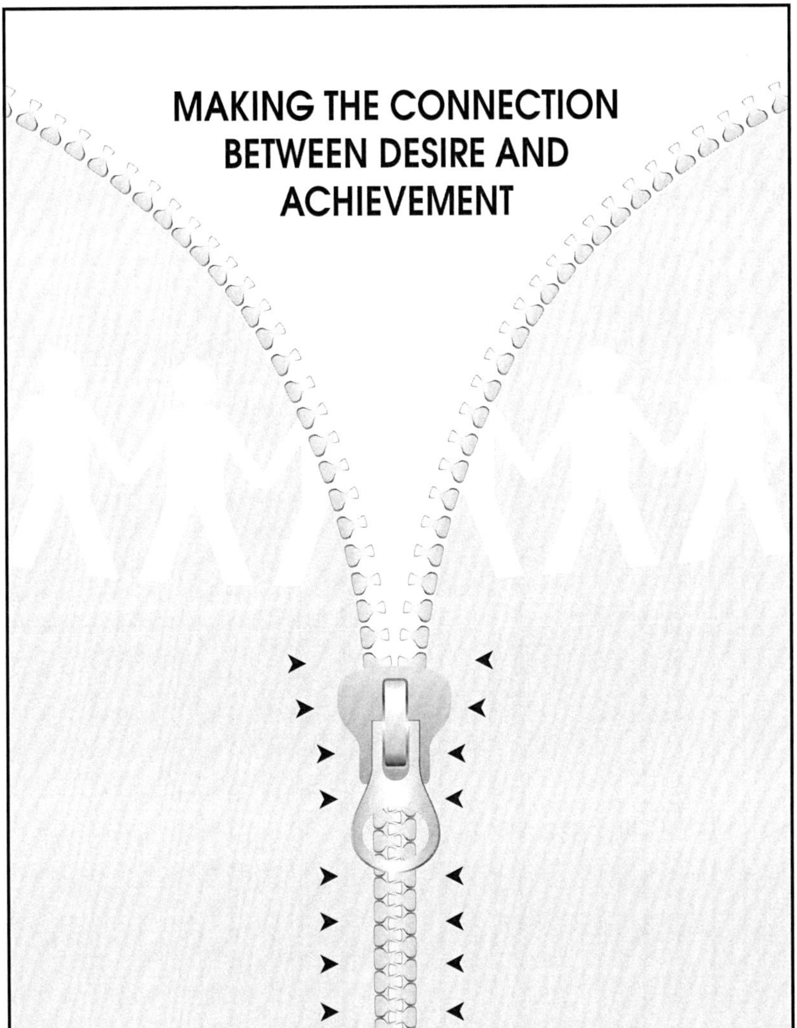

MAKING THE CONNECTION BETWEEN DESIRE AND ACHIEVEMENT

Desire

Achievement

CONNECTING YOUR BUSINESS PLAN AND YOUR BRANDING INTO ACTION

"Business is not financial science, it's about trading…buying and selling. It's about creating a product or service so good that people will pay for it."

Anita Roddick

CHAPTER 2

We can't talk about connecting your desires to infinite success without talking about your business plan, vision, mission and overall branding; taking it to market. As do most things in life, our lessons come from our experiences. The first thoughts we have on new ideas always end up with some kind of adjustment and tweaking.

Once you complete a business plan, you should also create a marketing plan that includes all facets of branding. You have to put your plan into action and make sure it all connects to your corporate identity, brand identity and brand image. Finally, you have to create your sales plan. Over the years I have seen many companies lump together or get

confused between the efforts of marketing vs. sales. The skill sets needed to design and drive both are vastly different and should be treated as such. This has become more prevalent over the years with social and media online marketing. Keeping up with the Joneses in business is becoming more and more taxing if you don't have experts surrounding you with the most current and relevant information. There's a lot to keep up with and how we market to our customers can be different depending on your trade as well as where your current and future customers shop for your services and products.

So let's dive in first with some basic, detailed definitions to set the stage for each topic and see how they all interconnect.

Defining **Business Plan** as:

1) A written document that describes in detail how a new business is going to achieve its goals. A business plan will lay out a written plan from a marketing, financial and operational viewpoint, connecting all your focus points and efforts in one clear direction and continual path. Sometimes a business plan is prepared for an established business that is moving in a new direction.

Defining **Mission Statement** as:

1) A written declaration of an organization's core purpose and focus that normally remains unchanged over time.
2) Properly crafted mission statements
    a. Serve as filters to separate what is important from what is not,

b. Clearly state which markets will be served and how, and
c. Communicate a sense of intended direction to the entire organization.

Defining **Vision Statement** as:

1) An aspirational description of what an organization would like to achieve or accomplish in the mid- or long-term. It is intended to serve as a clear guide for choosing current and future courses of action.

Defining **Marketing Plan** as:

1) A business document written for the purpose of describing the current market position of a business and its marketing strategy for the period covered by the plan. Marketing plans usually have a life of from one to five years.
2) Purpose of a Marketing Plan: The purpose of creating a marketing plan is to clearly show what steps will be undertaken to achieve the business' marketing objectives.

Defining **Sales Plan** as:

1) A plan containing an assessment of current sales for a product in a given region or market, a statement of sales objectives, strategies for achieving the stated sales objectives and resources available for achieving this goal. A sales plan may also assign particular sales representatives or other staff to particular roles or

territories, and may include a breakdown of who will focus on improving sales for which product.

Defining **Branding** as:

1) The process involved in creating a unique name and image for a product in the consumer's mind, mainly through advertising campaigns with a consistent theme.
2) Branding aims to establish a significant and differentiated presence in the market that attracts and retains loyal customers.
3) It is important to distinguish between corporate identity, brand identity and brand image:
    a. Corporate identity is concerned with the visual aspects of a company's presence.
    b. Brand identity is the total proposition that a company makes to consumers and the promise it makes.
    c. Brand image, on the other hand, is the totality of consumer perceptions about the brand, or how they see it, which may not coincide with the brand identity.

Defining **Viral** as:

1) Relating to or involving an image, video, piece of information, etc., that is circulated rapidly and widely from one Internet user to another.

Defining **Emotions** as:

1) A natural instinctive state of mind deriving from one's circumstances, mood or relationships with others.

Defining **Sharing** as:

1) Having a portion of (something) with another or others; giving; providing information on something; connecting.

CONNECTING YOUR BUSINESS PLAN, MISSION AND VISION

Let's face it, writing a business plan is just plan hard and very time consuming. However, it is a necessity to remain focused and have the ability to talk to bankers, investors, partners and more. Whether you are doing a full-blown, 100-page document or just getting started to write your ideas and thoughts down, you do have to include some basics. On the Internet, you can find several free templates and guides. In this chapter and section we are going to talk about the core components only. Don't think of this as an exercise or task but more as a road map to guide you and your team into the future. As you create the plan, you can go back and adjust as much as necessary.

I strongly encourage you to get lots of feedback from your circle of influence as well as your potential customers, clients and alliances. In Chapter 3 you will practice and deliver your 60-second pitches and introductions. This will allow you

to continually fine tune your message about your company, your brand and yourself. In Chapter 4 you will find more ways to add substance to your written plans as you complete detailed and specific research to ensure you are fully connecting in the manner you envisioned.

Now that you understand why you need a business plan and you've spent some time doing your homework gathering the information you need to create one, it's time to roll up your sleeves and get everything down on paper. The following will describe in detail the seven essential sections of a business plan: what you should include, what you shouldn't include, how to work the numbers and additional resources you can turn to for help. With that in mind, jump right in.

Business Plan Statement Core Elements*

1) Executive Summary

   Within the overall outline of the business plan, the executive summary will follow the title page. The summary should tell the reader what you want. This is very important. All too often, what the business owner desires is buried on page eight. Clearly state what you're asking for in the summary.

   The statement should be kept short and businesslike, probably no more than half a page. It could be longer, depending on how complicated the use of funds may be, but the summary of a business plan, like the summary of a loan application, is generally no longer than one page. Within that space, you'll need to provide a synopsis of your entire business plan. Key elements that should be included are:

a) Business concept. Describes the business, its product and the market it will serve. It should point out just exactly what will be sold, to whom and why the business will hold a competitive advantage.
b) Financial features. Highlights the important financial points of the business including sales, profits, cash flows and return on investment.
c) Financial requirements. Clearly states the capital needed to start the business and to expand. It should detail how the capital will be used, and the equity, if any, that will be provided for funding. If the loan for initial capital will be based on security instead of equity, you should also specify the source of collateral.
d) Current business position. Furnishes relevant information about the company, its legal form of operation, when it was formed, the principal owners and key personnel.
e) Major achievements. Details any developments within the company that are essential to the success of the business. Major achievements include items like patents, prototypes, location of a facility, any crucial contracts that need to be in place for product development, or results from any test marketing that has been conducted.

What are the bullet points of your executive summary?

✓ ____

✓ ____

✓ ____

✓ ____

✓ ____

2) Statement of Purpose

When writing your statement of purpose, don't waste words. If the statement of purpose is eight pages, nobody's going to read it because it'll be very clear that the business, no matter what its merits, won't be a good investment because the principals are indecisive and don't really know what they want. Make it easy for the reader to realize at first glance both your needs and capabilities.

What is the bullet point of your statement of purpose?

✓ ____

3) Business Description

a) The business description usually begins with a short description of the industry.
b) When describing the industry, discuss the present outlook as well as future possibilities.
c) You should also provide information on all the various markets within the industry, including any new products or developments that will benefit or adversely affect your business.

d) Base all of your observations on reliable data and be sure to footnote sources of information as appropriate. This is important if you're seeking funding; the investor will want to know just how dependable your information is, and won't risk money on assumptions or conjecture.

What are the bullet points of your business description?

✓ ______________________________

✓ ______________________________

✓ ______________________________

✓ ______________________________

4) Business Structure

When describing your business, the first thing you need to concentrate on is its structure. By structure, we mean the type of operation; i.e., wholesale, retail, food service, manufacturing or service-oriented. Also state whether the business is new or already established.

What are the bullet points of your business structure?

✓ ______________________________

✓ ______________________________

✓ ______________________________

✓ ______________________________

5) Legal Structure

In addition to structure, legal form should be reiterated once again. Detail whether the business is a sole proprietorship, partnership or corporation, who its principals are and what they will bring to the business.

What is your legal structure?

✓ ____

6) Business Support Systems

You should also mention who you will sell to, how the product will be distributed and the business's support systems. Support may come in the form of advertising, promotions and customer service.

What are your needed business support systems?

✓ ____
✓ ____
✓ ____
✓ ____

7) Describe Products or Services

The product description statement should be complete enough to give the reader a clear idea of your intentions. You may want to emphasize any unique features or variations from concepts that can typically be found in the industry.

a) Be specific in showing how you will give your business a competitive edge. For example, your business will be better because you will supply a full line of products:

   i) Competitor A doesn't have a full line. You're going to provide service after the sale.

   ii) Competitor B doesn't support anything he sells. Your merchandise will be of higher quality. You'll give a money-back guarantee.

   iii) Competitor C has the reputation for selling the best French fries in town; you're going to sell the best Thousand Island dressing.

How would you describe your products and services?

✓ ____

✓ ____

✓ ____

✓ ____

8) Description of Profit, Business Concept

"How can I turn a buck? And why do I think I can make a profit that way?" Answer that question for yourself, and then convey that answer in this section. Show how you will expand your business or be able to create something.

Explain the factors you think will make it successful, like the following:

a) It's a well-organized business.
b) It will have state-of-the-art equipment.
c) Its location is exceptional.
d) The market is ready for it.
e) It's a dynamite product at a fair price.

How do you describe your profit and overall business concept?

✓ ____
✓ ____
✓ ____
✓ ____

9) Define Your Market

Market strategies are the result of a meticulous market analysis. A market analysis forces the entrepreneur to become familiar with all aspects of the market so that the target market can be defined and the company can be positioned in order to garner its share of sales. A market analysis also enables the entrepreneur to establish pricing, distribution and promotional strategies that will allow the company to become profitable within a competitive environment. In addition, it provides an indication of the growth potential within the industry, and this will allow you to develop your own estimates for the future of your business.

Begin your market analysis by defining the market in terms of size, structure, growth prospects, trends and sales potential.

The total aggregate sales of your competitors will provide you with a fairly accurate estimate of the total potential market. Once the size of the market has been determined, the next step is to define the target market. The target market narrows down the total market by concentrating on segmentation factors that will determine the total addressable market--the total number of users within the sphere of the business's influence. The segmentation factors can be geographic, customer attributes or product-oriented.

How do you describe your market?

✓ ____

✓ ____

✓ ____

✓ ____

10) Is the Market Feasible

Once the target market has been detailed, it needs to be further defined to determine the total feasible market. This can be done in several ways, but most professional planners will delineate the feasible market by concentrating on product segmentation factors that may produce gaps

within the market. In the case of a microbrewery that plans to brew a premium lager beer, the total feasible market could be defined by determining how many drinkers of premium pilsner beers there are in the target market.

Is your market feasible? Why or why not?

✓ ______________________________

✓ ______________________________

✓ ______________________________

✓ ______________________________

11) Projecting Market Share

Arriving at a projection of the market share for a business plan is very much a subjective estimate. It's based not only on an analysis of the market but on highly targeted and competitive distribution, pricing and promotional strategies. For instance, even though there may be a sizable number of premium pilsner drinkers to form the total feasible market, you need to be able to reach them through your distribution network at a price point that's competitive, and then you have to let them know it's available and where they can buy it. How effectively you can achieve your distribution, pricing and promotional goals determines the extent to which you will be able to garner market share.

For a business plan, you must be able to estimate market share for the time period the plan will cover. In order to project market share over the time frame of the business plan, you'll need to consider two factors:

a) Industry growth which will increase the total number of users.
b) Conversion of users from the total feasible market.

What does your market share look like?

✓ ______________________________
✓ ______________________________
✓ ______________________________
✓ ______________________________

12) Positioning Your Business

A company's positioning strategy is affected by a number of variables that are closely tied to the motivations and requirements of target customers within as well as the actions of primary competitors. Before a product can be positioned, you need to answer several strategic questions such as:

a) How are your competitors positioning themselves?
b) What specific attributes does your product have that your competitors' don't?
c) What customer needs does your product fulfill?

How do you plan on positioning your product or services?

✓ ______________________________

✓ ______________________________

✓ ______________________________

✓ ______________________________

13) Define Pricing

How you price your product is important because it will have a direct effect on the success of your business. Though pricing strategy and computations can be complex, the basic rules of pricing are straightforward:

a) All prices must cover costs.
b) The best and most effective way of lowering your sales prices is to lower costs.
c) Your prices must reflect the dynamics of cost, demand, changes in the market and response to your competition.
d) Prices must be established to assure sales. Don't price against a competitive operation alone. Rather, price to sell.
e) Product utility, longevity, maintenance and end use must be judged continually, and target prices adjusted accordingly.
f) Prices must be set to preserve order in the marketplace.

How would you define your pricing?

✓ ____
✓ ____
✓ ____
✓ ____

14) Distribution

Distribution includes the entire process of moving the product from the factory to the end user. The type of distribution network you choose will depend upon the industry and the size of the market. A good way to make your decision is to analyze your competitors to determine the channels they are using, then decide whether to use the same type of channel or an alternative that may provide you with a strategic advantage. There are many ways to distribute your product and services: direct sales, manufacturer's sales representative, wholesale distributor, broker distribution, retail distributors or direct mail.

What are you plans for distribution, who and how?

✓ ____
✓ ____
✓ ____
✓ ____

15) Promotion Plan

With a distribution strategy formed, you must develop a promotion plan. The promotion strategy in its most basic form is the controlled distribution of communication designed to sell your product or service. In order to accomplish this, the promotion strategy encompasses every marketing tool utilized in the communication effort. This includes advertising, packaging, public relations, sales promotions and personal sales.

What are your promotional plans?

✓ ____

✓ ____

✓ ____

✓ ____

16) Sales Potential

Once the market has been researched and analyzed, conclusions need to be developed that will supply a quantitative outlook concerning the potential of the business. The first financial projection within the business plan must be formed utilizing the information drawn from defining the market, positioning the product, pricing, distribution and strategies for sales. The sales or revenue model charts the potential for the product, as well as the business, over a set period of time. Most business plans will project revenue for up to three years, although five-year projections are becoming increasingly popular among lenders.

When developing the revenue model for the business plan, the equation used to project sales is fairly simple. It consists of the total number of customers and the average revenue from each customer.

What is your sales potential?

✓ ______________________________________

✓ ______________________________________

✓ ______________________________________

✓ ______________________________________

17) Identify and Analyze Your Competition

The competitive analysis is a statement of the business strategy and how it relates to the competition. The purpose of the competitive analysis is to determine the strengths and weaknesses of the competitors within your market, strategies that will provide you with a distinct advantage, the barriers that can be developed in order to prevent competition from entering your market and any weaknesses that can be exploited within the product development cycle. *In Chapter 4, I discuss how to complete an S.W.O.T. analysis.*

Who are your competitors?

✓ ____

✓ ____

✓ ____

✓ ____

18) Design and Development Plan Section

The purpose of the design and development plan section is to provide investors with a description of the product's design, chart its development within the context of production, marketing and the company itself, and create a development budget that will enable the company to reach its goals.

There are generally three areas you'll cover in the development plan section:

a) Product Development
b) Market Development
c) Organizational Development

Each of these elements needs to be examined from the funding of the plan to the point where the business begins to experience a continuous income. Although these elements will differ in nature concerning their content, each will be based on structure and goals.

What are your elements of design for products and services?

✓ ____
✓ ____
✓ ____
✓ ____

19) Goals for Product Development

a) Technical and Marketing Aspects
b) Procedures
c) Scheduling and Costs
d) Development Budgets
e) Personnel
f) Assessing Risks

What are the bullet points of your applicable product development?

✓ ____
✓ ____
✓ ____
✓ ____

20) Operations and Management Section

The operations plan will highlight the logistics of the organization such as the various responsibilities of the management team, the tasks assigned to each division

within the company, and capital and expense requirements related to the operations of the business.

The financial tables that you'll develop within the operations plan include:

a) The Operating Expense Table
b) The Capital Requirements Table
c) The Cost of Goods Table

What does your organizational structure consist of?

✓ ____________________
✓ ____________________
✓ ____________________
✓ ____________________

21) Financial Statements Section

Financial data is always at the back of the business plan, but that doesn't mean it's any less important than up-front material such as the business concept and the management team. Astute investors look carefully at the charts, tables, formulas and spreadsheets in the financial section, because they know that this information is like the pulse, respiration rate and blood pressure in a human. It shows whether the patient is alive and what the odds are for continued survival.

a) Income Statements should include:
   i) Income

ii) Cost of Goods
iii) Gross Profit Margin
iv) Operating Expenses
v) Total Expenses
vi) Net Profit
vii) Depreciation
viii) Net Profit Before Interest
ix) Interest
x) Net Profit Before Taxes
xi) Taxes
xii) Profit After Taxes

b) Cash Flow Statements should include:
   i) Cash Sales
   ii) Receivables
   iii) Other Income
   iv) Total Income
   v) Material/Merchandise
   vi) Production Labor
   vii) Marketing/Sales
   viii) Research and Development
   ix) General and Administration
   x) Taxes
   xi) Loan Payment
   xii) Total Expenses
   xiii) Cash Flow
   xiv) Cumulative Cash Flow

c) Balance Sheet should include:
   i) Assets
      (1) Cash
      (2) Accounts Receivable
      (3) Inventory
      (4) Total Current Assets
   ii) Liabilities
      (1) Capital and Plant
      (2) Investment
      (3) Miscellaneous Assets
      (4) Total Long-Term Assets
      (5) Total Assets
   iii) Equity
      (1) Accounts Payable
      (2) Accrued Liabilities
      (3) Taxes
      (4) Total Current Liabilities
      (5) Long-Term Liabilities include:
         (a) Bonds Payable
         (b) Mortgage Payable
         (c) Notes Payable
         (d) Total Long-Term Liabilities
         (e) Total Liabilities

Have you completed your financial statements? If not, what is stopping you? What information is still needed?

✓ ____

✓ ____

CAN YOUR MARKETING MESSAGE GO VIRAL AND MAKE A FULL CONNECTION?

A basic human need and desire is to be heard and recognized. The desire to be liked and followed has been supersized in the world of marketing today. Have you heard the term "Going V?" No it's not V for victory, although many make the argument that once you go "Viral" in social media your entire game has changed, usually for the better. Making the connection and having the ability to have and or write content that goes viral is the name of the game in today's fast-paced, crazy race to visibility.

Everyone wants to have a successful viral campaign–it's the Holy Grail of marketing accomplishments and one of the biggest milestones. Making the connection to your current audience and potential future customers is certainly the goal. The phenomenon of viral marketing is fueled by the power of social platforms and the basic human need to be entertained, amused or enlightened. The Internet, which has changed everything, continues to change on a daily basis.

As humans, one of our natural instincts is our need to "share" and "connect" to others; online social media has become an acceptable and expected way to do this. It's how things and people are marketed and branded and how company messages and stories come to life. But I send a word of caution. You can't just say this "content" is going to go viral. Instead you must first connect your well-crafted message, story, commercial and video to your vision, your mission, who you are and why you are–that's still the key. We

all want to connect to "real" things, "real" people, "real" problems and "real" solutions.

Here are some questions you need to ask yourself:

1. How will my message resonate?
2. Will it engage my target audience?
3. Have I done the research needed to ensure my audience will tune in?
4. Does this message stay connected to my brand? My company's brand?

Playbook extra: Don't forget to ask yourself these questions with all your messages, not just the ones you have included in your marketing efforts. Every effort, every message written, every video, every blog, every networking event…stamp them with your brand and keep them basic, focused and consistent.

So let's break it down….

Infectious behavior: Virality isn't about luck; it's about creating clever, engaging content that's irresistible to consumers across all corners of the social media landscape.

Getting your brand noticed via social media grows more difficult with each passing day. Users upload 100 hours of video to YouTube every 60 seconds and share more than 4.75 billion pieces of content on Facebook every 24 hours. Add to that 500 million new Tweets per day, and chances of breaking through to a wider audience can seem virtually nonexistent.

Smart, savvy companies of all sizes are still exploding into the mainstream consciousness by creating campaigns that compel consumers to share content with their social graphs. Some are simply hilarious and some go straight to your heart, but they all set triggers in our heads.

Emotion is one factor that drives sharing. We see lots of funny stuff go viral on YouTube. Any emotion that fires us up–humor, awe and excitement, but also anger and anxiety–drives us to share.

Social media is also the great equalizer: Any company can cut through the clutter, regardless of brand awareness or marketing budget. All it takes is a clever idea and skillful execution.

THE CONNECTION BETWEEN SALES AND MARKETING

Understanding and making the connection yet separation between your sales and marketing efforts can be one of the crucial components to your long-term success as well as the timeline you have established to reach success. Of course, they are connected in many ways but should be delivered and driven by separate efforts that continually check in with one another. They walk hand in hand but with different bodies. I keep stressing this as there still seems to be confusion on this in almost every business I have worked with and for in the past as well as currently.

What is the difference between marketing and sales?

Do you know the difference between marketing and sales? Let's think about this question for a moment. Without marketing you would not have prospects or leads to follow up with, but yet without a good sales technique and strategy your closing rate may depress you. Marketing and sales should work simultaneously, but in most companies they are departments that don't even speak to each other.

If we break it down to the basics, marketing is everything you do to reach and persuade prospects and the sales process is everything you do to close the sale and get a signed agreement or contract. Both are necessary to the success of a business. You cannot do without either process. If you work to strategically combine both efforts you will experience a successful amount of business growth. However, by the same token if the efforts are unbalanced or departments don't communicate, it can detour business growth.

Your marketing should consist of strategies that you can use to measure your reach, and work to persuade your prospects that you are the company for them. It's the message that prepares the prospect for the sale. It could consist of advertising, public relations, social media, relationship marketing, brand marketing, viral marketing and direct mail.

The sales process consists of interpersonal interaction. It is often done by a one-on-one meeting, cold calls and networking. It's anything that engages you with the prospect or customer on a personal level rather than at a distance. Most the time the prospect or potential customer has been driven to you via marketing efforts.

I like to think of it like this: Your marketing efforts begin the process of the eight contacts or touch-points that studies show it takes to move a prospect or potential client to the close of the sale. If marketing is done effectively, you can begin to move that prospect from the status of a cold lead to a warm lead. When the prospect hits the "warm" level it's much easier for the sales professional or sales department to close the sale.

Studies have shown that it takes multiple contacts using both sales and marketing to move the prospect from one level to the next. That is why it is important that you develop a process that combines both sales and marketing. This will enable you to reach prospects at all three levels: cold, warm and hot. It's all about balance. Make sure that you've integrated both marketing and sales. They are not separate. If they are different departments, those departments must talk and communicate in order to be effective.

Are you unsure of how to integrate your marketing and sales?

PLAYBOOK ACTION: Take a few moments and divide your prospect lists and database into categories of cold, warm and hot leads. Then sit down and identify a strategy on how to proceed with each individual group.

Cold List:

____
____
____
____
____
____
____
____

Warm List:

____
____
____
____
____
____

Hot List: What are you waiting for? Go make the sales call and close the deal. Who is on your list?

____

____

____

____

____

____

For example, you could try the following methods of contact:

a) Cold Lead Strategy: Send out a direct mailing or offer them a special promotion.
b) Who can you send one of these to, from your list above?

   ____

   ____

   ____

   ____

c) Warm Lead Strategy: Try a follow-up call, send out a sales letter, or schedule a special seminar or training session to get all of your warm leads together.
d) Who can you do one of these with from your list above?

   ____

   ____

   ____

   ____

Once you've moved your prospect to the "warm" level, it's time to proceed in closing the sale. Call it passing the baton, if you'd like. This will be easier to do if you somehow engage the prospect. You can do this by conducting a one-on-one call, making a presentation or presenting a proposal, estimate or contract.

What if you are uncomfortable with the sales or marketing process?

An alternative that often proves successful is to partner with someone who possesses the talents that you feel you lack. If you are stronger in marketing, find someone who understands the sales process. If you are better at sales, find someone who can help you strengthen the message, create marketing materials that sell and give you tactics and ideas. If you don't work in a company that has both departments and you are working solo you can do this by creating a partnership, subcontracting or hiring that talent. The key to success in marketing and in sales is balance and their full connection.

ACTION IS CALLING: Review the Business Plan, Mission, Vision, Marketing Plan, Branding and Sales Plan into Action

1) What is your biggest take away-action plan for your business plan beginning or update?

____

____

____

____

2) Does your Mission Statement fit your current state and describe what you, your department, your company represents? If not, how can you adjust?

____

____

____

____

3) Does your Vision Statement give you a clear look into the future and how you want to be described? If not, how can you adjust?

____

____

____

____

4) Do you have separate marketing and sales plans? If not, how can you begin to pull this together? What time frame? What are some bullet points you can capture now while this is fresh in your mind?

____

____

____

____

5) When you review your branding components, are your messages clear and catchy? Do they have the right elements to go viral?

Clear?____

Catchy?_______________________________________

Memorable?____________________________________

6) Does your Business Plan connect to your Mission, your Vision, your Marketing, your Sales and your overall Branding and where your opportunities lie?

____

____

____

____

____

*Sources: Lori A. Parch, *The Small Business Encyclopedia, Business Plans Made Easy,* and *Start Your Own Business; Entrepreneur Magazine.*

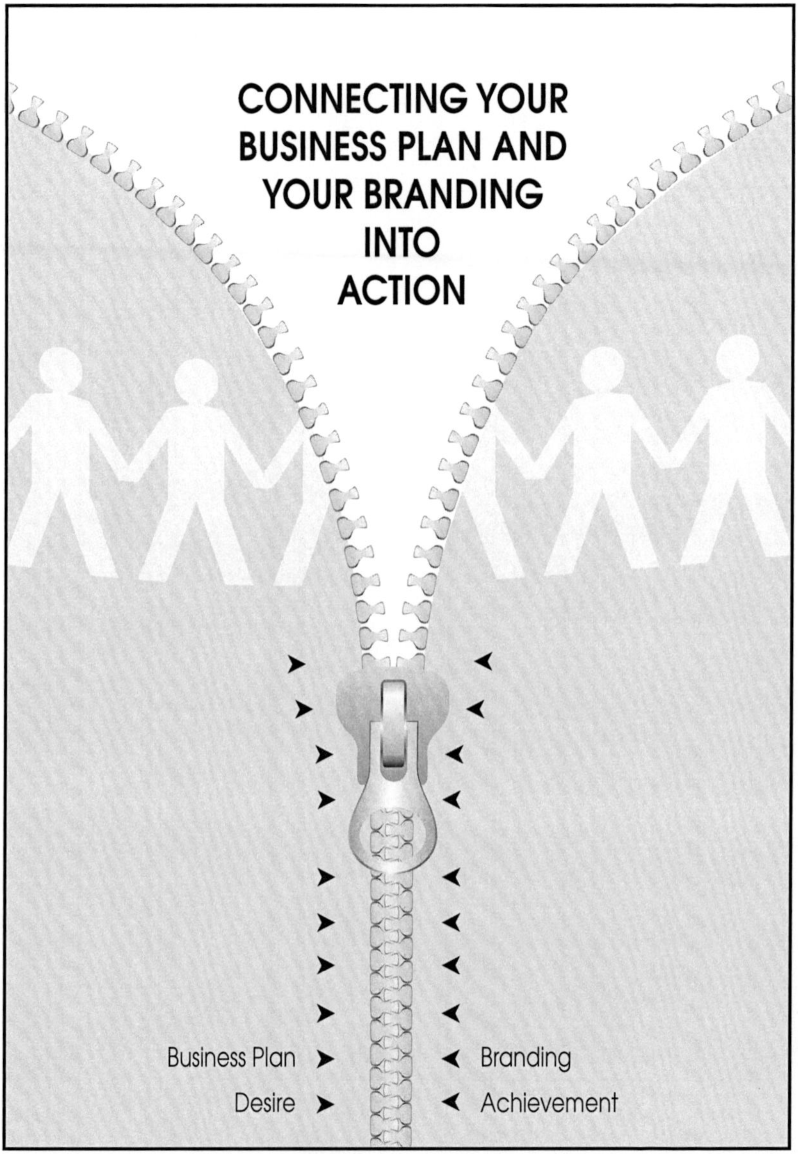

CONNECTING YOUR BUSINESS PLAN AND YOUR BRANDING INTO ACTION

Business Plan ➤ ◀ Branding

Desire ➤ ◀ Achievement

60 SECONDS TO CONNECT

"It's important to start with a simple idea, it might be really hard to execute, but it should be very easy to explain."

Steve Hafner, CEO of Kayak

CHAPTER 3

It doesn't matter if you're mingling with friends, or you're at the airport, or attending a networking event or entrepreneurship conference, or you just happen to know someone who *knows* someone who can help you take your company to the next level. Invariably, someone will ask: "What do you do for a living?" Or "Who do you work for?" Or "What is your company all about?"

This is where you take the opportunity to make the "connection" not necessarily the "sell." People connect to those they "get," those they relate to. When you are authentic, intriguing and passionate, people want to know more about you and your company. This is the now infamous "elevator pitch" (introduction, your 60-second connection and sometimes your value proposition). That's what it was all created for–your time and ability to quickly "connect" and make a lasting impression and connection for future opportunities.

Defining **Introduction** as:

1) A formal presentation of one person to another individually or within a group; point of referencing business or self.

WHY: Connecting Your 60 Seconds to Your Goal

What is your goal when you do an introduction? Please stop and quickly write it down. What is your purpose? Please do this before you read further.

____

____

____

____

- The elevator speech
- The pitch
- Your 60 seconds for your business networking event introduction
- Your value proposition

HOW: To Connect in Your 60 Seconds

Whatever you call your "spill" isn't the point. The point is make it clear, make it concise, make it memorable and most importantly make it re-memorable. If you have various segments and types of services or offerings, then you should

have various types of introductions to go along with each. Your introductions should always be adjusted based on the audience you are speaking to or in front of.

TIPS for the Connection

1. The next time you attend an event that allows for group round table introductions, very intently listen to each person's 60 seconds. You may be amazed to hear how many people stumble or ramble through theirs and forget the introduction's key purpose. The result? They don't leave you with what they were hoping you'd take away from their intro.

2. While attending networking groups, I always take note of those in duplicate trades giving their introductions. It's always interesting to see how well each business representative adjusts their content as the introductions continue. Are they prepared to adjust based on what they heard their competitor say? Or do they simply repeat the same type of information?

3. Remember that the introduction is your one chance to be remembered by several potential customers at once. It's like going on Google and shopping for a new car; you can pull the options up and compare. The one that stands out and gives the most product/value differentiation is the one you will more than likely remember and investigate further.

4. <u>The ability to pivot and connect your language to those around you can and will give you the edge.</u> Listening to attendees and being ready to adjust your spill are key points as well. Your goal is to resonate long term to your fellow networkers.

ACTION IS CALLING: Review the Playbook and Your Ability to Connect in 60 Seconds

1. Record yourself right now on your phone, computer or camera.
2. Immediately go back and listen to it.
3. Write down what you heard–what you *really* heard (bullet points).
    a. ______________________________
    b. ______________________________
    c. ______________________________
    d. ______________________________
    e. ______________________________
4. What was your take-away? Write down the first thing you remember, don't over-think this.
    a. ______________________________
5. Did you do it in 60 seconds? How long was it really?
    a. ______________________________
6. How was your tone? Did you sound happy, smiling and passionate, like an expert? Or were you monotone, dry, non-emotional and disconnected?
    a. ______________________________

7. How was your speed? Meaning your speech speed. Too fast, too slow or just right?
    a. ______________________
8. How was your diction? Did you clearly enunciate all your words? Did you use words that are natural to you or try and sound more "intellectual" than you normally would?
    a. ______________________
9. Did you say your name; first and last?
    a. ______________________
10. Did you say your company's name? At the opening and closing?
    a. ______________________
11. Did you say how long you have been in business?
    a. ______________________
12. Did you say what you do; your company's big-picture focus?
    a. ______________________
13. Did you say why you do what you do? What's the connection? (Great video to watch from Simon Sinek, author of *Start with Why*, during a TED Talk http://www.ted.com/talks/simon_sinek_how_great_leaders_inspire_action)
    a. ______________________
14. Did you describe a problem and explain the services you and your company offer to solve this?
    a. ______________________
15. Did you differentiate yourself from your perceived competitors? Don't mention a competitor's name, but

highlight something that makes you stand out from the rest. Never, ever bash or put down your competitors.

a. ______________________________

16. What point did you want to make? And did you hear this loud and clear? If not, then you weren't clear or maybe didn't even say it.

    a. ______________________________
    b. ______________________________
    c. ______________________________

17. Next, have a friend, a partner or a co-worker listen to what you recorded and ask them to tell you what they heard.

    a. ______________________________

18. Did it match what you wanted them to hear? Can they tell others what you do? Can they tell others what your company does? Do they know how to refer you?

    a. ______________________________
    b. ______________________________

START AND CONNECT WITH THE END IN MIND

Write down the purpose or your goal when making an introduction. I know you wrote this down when the chapter opened but write it down again and then go back and re-read what you wrote earlier. Are the two statements of purpose different? Why or why not?

✓ ____
____
____

Moving Forward Tips and Reminders

Question: How do you know you said what you intended?

Answer: Ask those around you to repeat what they heard.

Practice! Practice, practice and rehearse some more. Your introduction should flow as easily as your name. Your passion and conviction should be clearly heard as well.

Three Connection Points

1. What do you sound like now?
   a. ____________________
2. What do you want to sound like in the future?
   a. ____________________
3. Why is this "connection" important?
   a. ____________________

60-SECOND Full Connection Check Points

✓ If you ask someone to introduce you to an audience and they nail every point you wanted to make and they do not have any affiliation to your company--<u>then you are fully connected</u>.

✓ If 10 out of 10 people in a group can do your 60 seconds and again nail everything you wanted to say and have them hear–<u>then you are fully connected</u>.

- ✓ If you received a referral from someone outside your company and you asked the prospect what it is they understand you do and who you are and they nail it–<u>then you are fully connected</u>.

If you don't fully connect in your 60 seconds, you may have lost another opportunity to be re-memorable and/or to connect in the future. Just like in football, the last Hail Mary of the game can take you to the win or into overtime. Your 60 seconds is your pass, you are the quarterback and the person or group you are talking to represents the potential receiver. If the time runs out during the pass and you don't make the connection with your receiver, the game is over. There are no do-overs when the clock runs out. Don't let your clock run out before making a connection–or your contract may not be renewed.

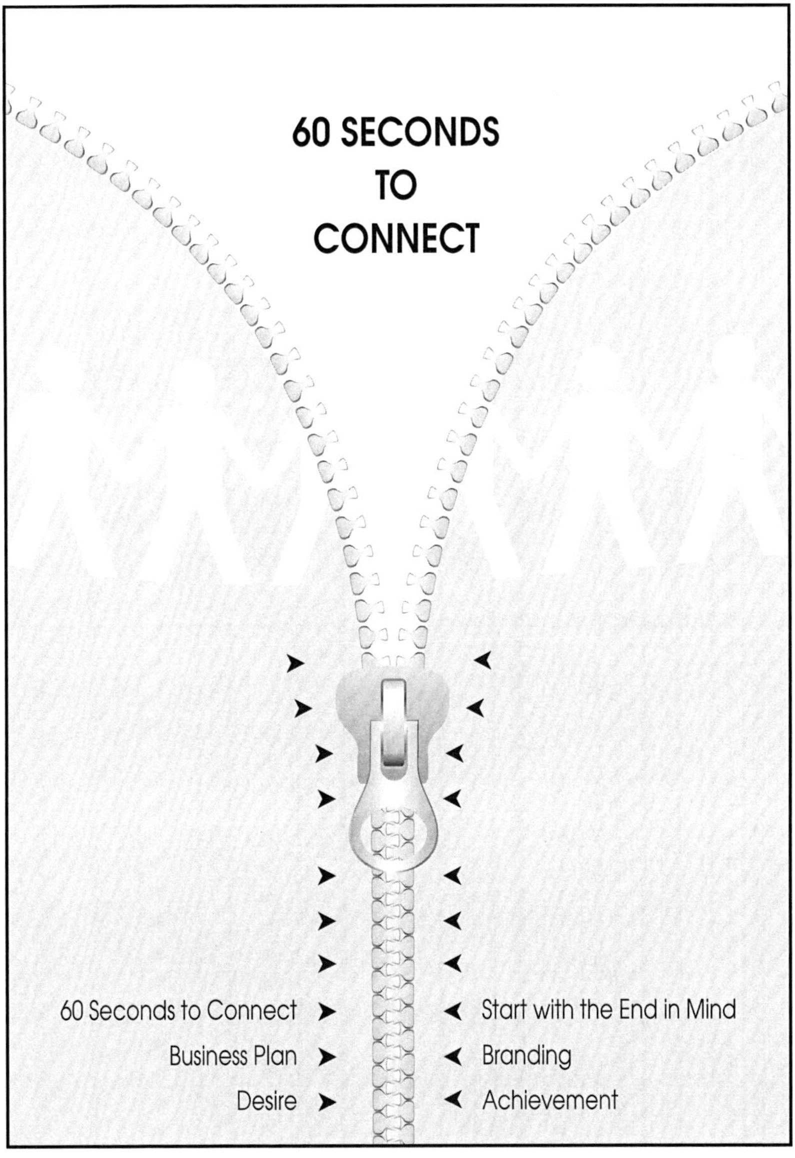

60 SECONDS TO CONNECT

60 Seconds to Connect	Start with the End in Mind
Business Plan	Branding
Desire	Achievement

USING VARIOUS LEVELS OF RESEARCH TO CONNECT AND GROW

"If we knew what it was we were doing, it would not be called research, would it?

Albert Einstein

CHAPTER 4

"Research?" you may be asking yourself. Why is there a chapter dedicated to research as it relates to being connected? Research can be a time-consuming task but an important activity to becoming fully connected. In this case I am asking you to dive into research in a variety of ways as you move forward in this *Connection* book. However, doing research isn't enough. It's what we do with the data and moving it into an analytic phase that counts. This is where the connections are made.

Defining **Research** as:

1) The systematic investigation into and study of materials and sources in order to establish facts and reach new conclusions.

Defining **Competitor** as:

1) An organization that is engaged in commercial or economic growth in competition.

Defining **Data** as:

1) Facts and statistics collected together for reference or analysis.

Defining **Analytic** as:

1) Pertaining to or proceeding by analysis.
2) Skilled in or habitually using analysis.

CONNECTING RESEARCH ON SELF, COMPETITORS, CLIENTS AND POTENTIAL CUSTOMERS

Let's dig deeper into the various types of research intended for our Connections Playbook. The following paragraphs target a variety of individuals or stages in business; thus the reference to research. For specific information, feel free to jump to the applicable areas.

- Research using S.W.O.T analysis
- Research using Google search
- Research with the use of online reports
- Research using Social Networks
- Research by talking to your customers
- Research by attending conferences
- Research through your suppliers
- Research and hire from your competitors
- Research who your competitors are hiring
- Research with use of surveys
- Research and go directly to your competitors

Competitors are out there and they're hungry for your customers. While it might seem unfair, given everything else you need to keep on top of in building up your business, you might want to consider putting some time and energy into keeping tabs on your competition or even making a strategic alliance. By monitoring competitors on an on-going basis you become familiar with behavior patterns and can start to anticipate what they will be likely to do next, which helps businesses like yours gain competitive intelligence. You can then plan your own strategies so that you keep your customers and win (not steal) customers away from competitors. In other words, keeping tabs on your competition is a great strategy for growing your business.

CONNECTING RESEARCH THROUGH A S.W.O.T ANALYSIS

Making a calculated strategic alignment with your competitor can also dramatically grow your business and exposure. When you align (connect) with others you can take on larger pieces of business that were previously out of your reach. Completing a traditional SWOT analysis is one of the most effective ways to not only research yourself but also your competition and potential strategic partners.

A SWOT analysis is commonly used in marketing and business in general as a method of identifying opposition for a new venture or strategy. Short for Strengths, Weaknesses, Opportunities and Threats, this allows you to identify all of the positive and negative elements that may affect any new proposed actions.

This analysis leads to business awareness and is the cornerstone of any successful strategic plan. It is impossible to accurately map out a small business's future without first evaluating it from all angles, which includes an exhaustive look at all internal and external resources and threats. A SWOT accomplishes this in four straight-forward steps that rookies and seasoned business owners and executives alike can understand and embrace.

The SWOT analysis enables companies to identify the positive and negative influencing factors inside and outside of a company or organization. Besides businesses, other organizations, in areas such as community health and development and education have found much use in its guiding principles. The key role of SWOT is to help develop a full awareness of all factors that may affect strategic planning and decision making, a goal that can be applied to most any aspect of industry.

SWOT is meant to act primarily as an assessment technique, though its lengthy record of success among many businesses makes it an invaluable tool in project management.

A good SWOT analysis serves as a dashboard to your product or services and when done correctly can help you to navigate and implement a sound strategy for your business regardless of company size or sector. I continue to revisit mine every year to keep it updated due to constant shifts in market trends. It's a crisp and simple way to communicate the most important aspects of my brand.

Performing a SWOT analysis is a great way to improve business operations and decision making. It allows you to identify the key areas where your organization is performing at a high level, as well as areas that need work. Some small business owners make the mistake of thinking about these sorts of things informally, but by taking the time to put together a formalized SWOT analysis, you can come up with ways to better capitalize on your company's strengths and improve or eliminate weaknesses.

While the business owner should certainly be involved in creating a SWOT analysis, it could be much more helpful to include other team members in the process.

A SWOT analysis focuses entirely on the four elements included in the acronym, allowing companies to identify the forces influencing a strategy, action or initiative. Knowing these positive and negative impacting elements can help companies more effectively communicate what elements of a plan need to be recognized.

When drafting a SWOT analysis, individuals typically create a table split up into four columns so as to list each impacting element side-by-side for comparison. Strengths and weaknesses won't typically match listed opportunities and threats, though some correlation should exist since they're tied together in some way.

Once you've identified your risks, you can then decide whether it is most appropriate to 1) eliminate the internal weakness by assigning company resources to fix the problems, or 2) reduce the external threat by setting the threatened component aside until you've strengthened your business.

Internal factors

The first two letters in the acronym signifying Strengths and Weaknesses refer to internal factors, which means the resources and experience readily available to you. Examples of areas typically considered include:

- Financial resources, such as funding, sources of income and investment opportunities.
- Physical resources, such as your company's location, facilities and equipment.
- Human resources, such as employees, volunteers and target audiences.
- Current processes, such as employee programs, department hierarchies and software systems.

When it comes to listing strengths and weaknesses, individuals shouldn't try to sugarcoat or glaze over inherent weaknesses or strengths. Identifying factors both good and bad is important in creating a thorough SWOT analysis.

"Using the SWOT analysis has, more than once, saved me from myself, keeping me from taking on projects that would likely have been too much for my small company," said Elizabeth Veliz, owner of Adelante HR Solutions.

External factors

Every company, organization and individual is influenced and affected by external forces. Whether connected directly or indirectly to an opportunity or threat, each of these factors is important to take note of and document. External factors typically reference things you or your company do not control, such as:

- Market trends, focusing on new products and technology or shifts in audience needs.

- Economic trends, based on local, national and international financial trends.
- Funding, from donations, legislation or other foundations.
- Demographics, involving a target audience's age, race, gender and culture.

"We used a SWOT analysis to identify a new market opportunity in small manufacturers that needed ink-on-paper projects," said Martha Forman, owner of Marketing by Design. "This provided organic, non-disruptive growth." On the other hand, Glenn Smith, owner of Kayaking Creative Trips, noted that a SWOT analysis helped his company fully analyze its pricing structure, since faulty pricing would have been a threat to the company's success.

Sample SWOT: SWOT Analysis template with some examples of questions you can answer:

STRENGTHS (internal)	WEAKNESSES (internal)
✓ Your specialist marketing expertise. ✓ An innovative product or service. ✓ Location of your business. ✓ Quality processes and procedures.	✓ Lack of marketing expertise. ✓ Similar products or services (i.e., in relation to your competitors). ✓ Location of your business.

✓ Other aspect of your business that adds value to your product or service.	✓ Poor quality goods or services. ✓ Damaged reputation.
OPPORTUNITIES (external)	THREATS (external)
✓ A developing market such as the Internet. ✓ Mergers, joint ventures or strategic alliances. ✓ Moving into new market segments that offer improved profits. ✓ A new international market. ✓ A market vacated by an ineffective competitor.	✓ A new competitor in your home market. ✓ Price wars with competitors. ✓ A competitor has a new, innovative product or service. ✓ Competitors have superior access to channels of distribution. ✓ Taxation is introduced on your product or service.

The SWOT analysis is a simple, albeit comprehensive strategy in identifying not only the weaknesses and threats of a plan, but also the strengths and opportunities available through it. While an excellent brainstorming tool, the four-cornered analysis prompts entities to examine and execute strategies in

a more balanced way. However, it is not the only factor in developing a business strategy.

The exercise alone won't identify the key value drivers of your business. Planning without first knowing your goals and the metrics by which you will measure your progress toward achieving those goals is inefficient and misguided.

When SWOT is used in conjunction with other analysis models, these frameworks for strategic thinking are well worth your time and should guide your decision making and the full connection to what, when and how you should move forward.

HOW TO USE RESEARCH TO CONNECT

Listed below are several ways you can complete this research and make sure you are fully connecting to all the opportunities and possibilities.

Someone on your staff can do the research or you can hire a consultant who specializes in various types of research. Hiring a firm can save you or your employees the time needed to conduct research on your competitors. You can also employ several techniques to get the job done virtually for free. Here are 10 tips from entrepreneurs and small business owners on how you can start gathering information on your competitors.

1. Research Using Google Search

There's no doubt that any research project these days should begin with a simple Google search or visiting your competitor's website. But there are also a variety of tools either supplied by Google or that relate to Google's search results and AdWords campaigns that might give you interesting insights into your competition. A comparison-shopping website for credit card processing uses the following tools to keep an eye on competition:

SpyFu: A great resource to research what keywords and AdWords our competitors are buying.

Google Trends: Helpful when you want to stay on top of the latest news in your industry, compare your company to others and see where people who come to your site go.

Google Alerts: Great for learning what your competitors are up to. (P.S. Don't forget to set up an alert on your own company to see if anyone else is talking about you.)

2. Research with the Use of Online Reports

There are great, inexpensive online resources for checking up on your competitors. I recommend routinely tracking what the industry analyst firms like Gartner are reporting about your industry, as well as trade associations and advocacy groups. Becky Sheetz-Runkle, author of *Sun Tzu for*

Women: The Art of War for Winning in Business, was quoted saying "These organizations are doing research and studies that evaluate the people who are and should be your competitors. What are they telling you about where the industry is trending? Where are the unmet market needs that you can fill?"

Other resources you can use to dig up information on your competitors include: Alexa, Compete, Keyword Spy, Hoovers and Reference USA.

3. Research Using Social Networking

Of course, given how companies are increasingly using social networking sites like Facebook, LinkedIn and Twitter as marketing outlets these days, you might be able to pick up interesting facts about your competition—and maybe even your own company—just by tuning in. I regularly monitor Tweets, Facebook posts and blogs for mentions about competitors. It's an easy, cost-effective way to stay in tune with and in the know about the public's sentiment regarding competing companies. In a similar vein, I track my competition by keeping a very close eye on review sites, such as Yelp and Citysearch. You scour through reviews to find mentions of your competitors' deals, and then target that particular Yelper or Citysearcher's other favorite businesses so you're always one step ahead of the competition. Even if your competition isn't social media savvy, it's a good bet that they produce newsletters—either e-mail or print varieties—that you can sign up for to get the latest and greatest news and updates on things like new products or services they are introducing and what events they might be attending.

4. Research by Talking to Your Customers

When it comes to identifying sources of information about your competition, don't skip over the obvious ones—like your customers. Speaking with customers is one of the best (and cheapest) ways of gathering real information on competitors. Whenever you win a new customer, find out who they used before, and why they switched to you (i.e., the reason they were dissatisfied with their previous supplier). Do the same when you lose a customer—identify what they preferred about your competitor. If you gather enough of these stories you'll get a very clear idea on what competitors are offering that customers view as preferable. You can then adjust your own offering to beat that of the competitor.

Colin Taylor, owner of Purpose in Profits, is known for focus on getting business owners to dial into the feedback they get from their current client base. Before he gives his suggestions and recommendations for improvement with growth, he conducts a business optimization review that includes customer-based research and interviews. His survey digs into the basics but it reveals priceless information. He teaches to never assume you know what your clients or customers would say and do say about you to others. Simply put: stop and take a pulse check to ensure the perceptions are in line with reality.

Here are some sample questions.

- How did you first hear about our company?
- Why did you buy in the first place?
- Is there anything I offer that in your opinion is unique compared to the competition?
- What is it that I do that makes me stand out from the competition?
- What are your biggest frustrations with my company?
- What three things could I improve upon?
- If you had a magic wand, what one thing would you like me to provide or do for you?
- From what sources do you get your information (newspapers, magazines, blogs, podcasts, radio shows, trade press, etc.)?
- How often would you like to be contacted with new information?
- Do you prefer being contacted by phone, mail or email?
- On a scale of 1 to 10, how likely is it that you would refer me to a friend or colleague?

5. Research by Attending Conferences

Attending industry trade shows and conferences—as well as joining industry associations—can be a great way to learn about who your competitors are and what they're offering. Make sure to visit competitors' booths while you are there and observe their interactions with customers. Pick up literature and check out the quality of their products.

6. Research Through Your Suppliers

If you work in an industry where you share the same suppliers as your competitors, it could pay to ask them some simple questions. Talk to your suppliers and spend time getting to know them. While they may not tell you what your competition ordered or their volume, ask better questions. For example, if you ask them how many units of a certain product have been pre-ordered for the next month, you might find out not only what your competition may have ordered, but what other products your supplier might be bringing in as a result.

7. Research and Hire from Your Competitors

Another strategy is to hire employees away from competing firms—especially sales people—and team up with a competitor's partners. No one knows more about the inside of those organizations than the employees. Find out all that you can about how these companies operate, and more importantly, what's on the horizon for them? Where are they taking their business? What markets are they venturing into? How are they leveraging innovation to cut costs and advance productivity? Where is the highest level of dissatisfaction with their products or services? No one has more and better intelligence when it comes to sales than disgruntled sales people.

8. Research Who Your Competitors are Hiring

You can also learn something by studying the kinds of jobs your competitors are looking to fill. For example, if a

company is hiring a programmer, they will include information about exactly what technologies the candidates need to know, which tells you what they use. Also look at what positions they are hiring—if they're looking for a patent attorney, they could be working on some big new inventions. If they're hiring for several HR positions, they may be preparing to expand overall.

9. Research with Use of Surveys

If you're interested in getting a comprehensive report of all the players in your industry, you might consider conducting a survey. You can put together a quick, meaningful survey via Survey Monkey for the cost of your time or a minimal fee. You can also hire larger, well known firms such as Gallup to conduct the surveys. The key to a successful survey is the questions you ask. The right questions give you the type of answers you seek and right information will allow you to confirm or pivot your strategies. The survey results allow you to put a solid plan into action.

10. Research and Go Directly to Your Competitors

Once you have done enough research to identify who your competitors are, you might want to try an old-school tactic to take it from there: Just call them up and ask away. One of the best ways to research competition is to call them and ask whatever you'd like. You'd be surprised how often companies will tell you everything you'd like to learn over the phone, especially if the question is phrased in a context that makes sense. For example, if you want to know how many people work there, you can say "I'm looking for individualized attention, and my fear is that your organization is too large and I'll get lost in the shuffle. How many coaches do you have on staff? Oh, wow, that's quite a few. How much support staff do you need for a team that size?" This approach has served me very well.

Bottom line: Research and then research some more, analyze your data and become friends with your competitors. You never know when the perfect strategic alignment and opportunity may come along.

ACTION IS CALLING: Review the Playbook Using Various Levels of Research to Connect and Grow

Set your goals high. If you want to grow, you have to know who you are, who you are dealing with and where you want to go in both the short term and the long term. The picture moves from foggy to clear as you do your internal and external research. Your Playbook action plan is to complete an outline that includes the list in this chapter. Start with the ones you are most comfortable with first and then keep digging to deepen your connection to your data, your analytics and your final solutions.

Action:

1. Over the next 30 days I will complete research on ___________ by using _____________ as the connection tool.
2. Over the next 90 days I will complete research on __________ by using _______________as the connection tool
3. Over the next six months I will complete research on __________ by using _______________as the connection tool.
4. Over the next year I will complete research on ___________ by using _____________as the connection tool.

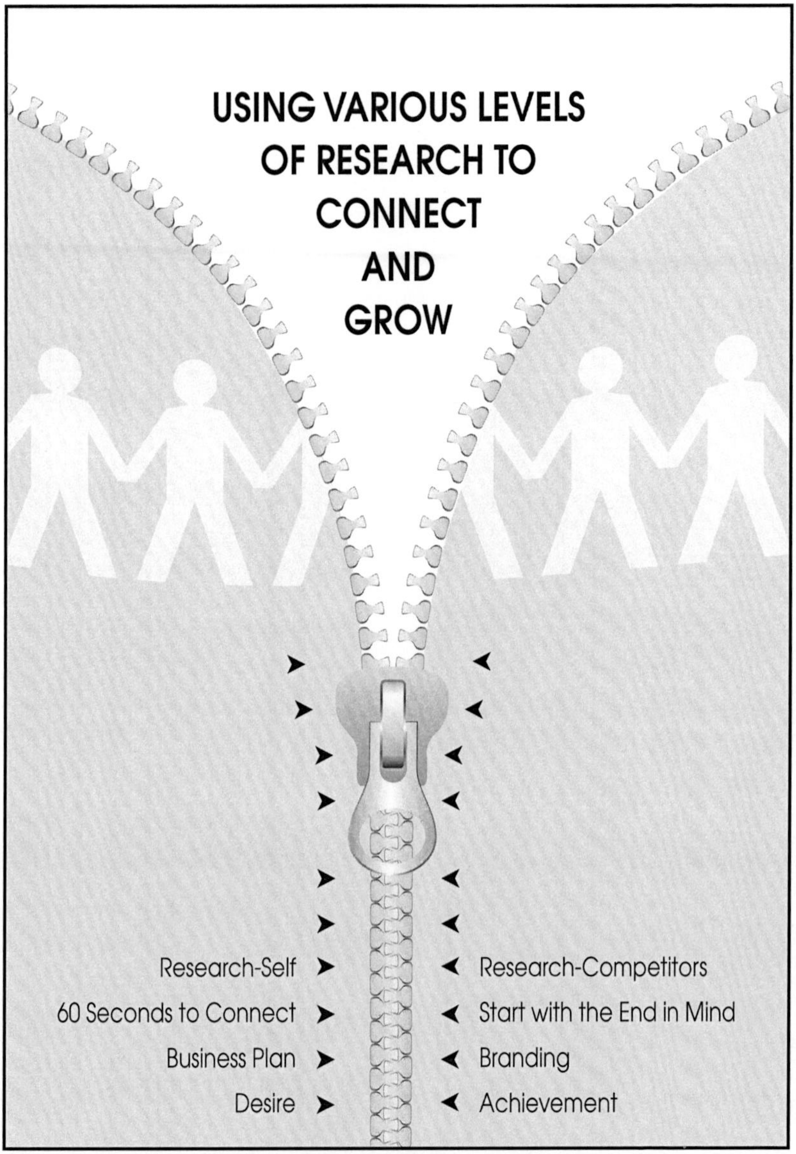

USING VARIOUS LEVELS OF RESEARCH TO CONNECT AND GROW

Research-Self ➤	◄ Research-Competitors
60 Seconds to Connect ➤	◄ Start with the End in Mind
Business Plan ➤	◄ Branding
Desire ➤	◄ Achievement

CONNECTING YOUR COLLEAGUES AND STRATEGIC ALLIANCES BY NETWORKING

"If you do not seek out allies and helpers, then you will be isolated and weak."

Sun Tzu, *The Art of War*

CHAPTER 5

Making the ongoing connection between the acts of networking internally and externally should be one of the key activities when working with our colleagues; finding those appropriate strategic partners with whom to align ourselves and our companies.

Finding those colleagues and alliances that complete rather than compete with you is key. It is an intersection we all must face and cross at some point in our careers. I encourage you to make that connection and cross that intersection sooner rather than later. When we build alliances and business partnerships, everyone benefits from respecting and integrating each other's differences rather than trying to override them. At the same time, we can embrace the similarities and raise them to even greater heights.

I can't tell you how many times I've been in a meeting or networking group with several individuals who are bright, creative and talented but who get stuck in their creative ideas and strategic initiatives. Keep in mind that collaborative efforts can always assist you with big breakthroughs and clarity.

Defining **Colleague** as:

1) A person with whom one works, especially in a profession or business.

Defining **Strategic Alliance** as:

1) An agreement between two or more parties to pursue a set of agreed upon objectives needed while remaining independent organizations. This form of cooperation lies between Mergers & Acquisition (M&A) and organic growth.

Defining **Networking** as:

1) A supportive system of sharing information and services among individuals and groups having a common interest.

THE COLLEAGUE CONNECTION

Your relationships with your colleagues are important. Good workplace relationships can help you do your job better. They can make going to work every day enjoyable. Bad relationships with colleagues can distract you and can turn a so-so job into a nightmare. These actions will help you have good relationships with your colleagues:

1. **Respect Your Colleagues**: Respect is the foundation of all good relationships, including those you have with your colleagues. Do your best to avoid offending those with whom you work. Of course, there will be the occasional prickly co-worker who is easily offended. There's little you can do about that.

2. **Listen More than Talk**: Whether you're asking questions or offering solutions, networking can be a transformative experience. Conversations held need to be in equal parts. Be very aware of your speaking part and engagement. Conversations must be two way, meaning listen more than you talk. When you talk more than you listen you can and will turn others off AND become disconnected.

3. **Ask Questions:** When networking or in conversations with others be fully engaged and aware of how many times you are answering questions vs. asking questions. The more you ask and probe in engaging conversations, the stronger the relationships you will build vs. risking tearing them down and becoming unplugged.

4. **Attend Business Events**: In today's world of networking, there are a number of opportunities for you to share ideas and gain the knowledge you need to advance your career and/or business. Through company conferences and webinars, tradeshows and various business affiliations, you can connect with peers who share your professional interests and meet new colleagues within your diverse community of management professionals.

THE NETWORK AND STRATEGIC ALLIANCE CONNECTION

Networking allows you to brand yourself and your company. Networking is the traditional way to get and stay connected, but make sure the events you choose to participate in have goals too. A networking event isn't as much about getting more business as it is staying in front of your business, keeping your knowledge and awareness in tune. It's about staying ahead of and being proactive about the "ever-changing" economy and market conditions. If you only live in the moment, you can never look ahead to the future.

A full networking connection is one that includes attendance for various reasons:

1. **Branding**: Maintaining the image and being the face of the company. Making sure you and your company are top of mind when someone needs the type of services or product you offer.

    a. What does your branding image look like?

    ____

    ____

    ____

    b. How would your brand be described by others?

    ____

    ____

    ____

2. **Prospecting**: Making new connections that could lead to additional business. Connecting

with those you already know who use and need the type of services or product you offer.

a. Who is at the top of your list to meet?

____

____

b. Who do you know that can introduce you to them?

____

____

____

c. What product or service are they using now that you can offer?

____

____

____

3. **Education**: Staying connected to your industry, the hottest tips and topics related to your field or those of your clients. Continuing education and fueling the mind keeps you from becoming stagnant.

   a. What was the last industry related conference or meeting you attended? What did you learn from it?

   ____

   ____

   ____

4. **Research**: Looking at what your perceived competitors are doing. Meeting top potential associates and strategic alliances. Staying connected to the market trends and economic conditions.

a. Who do you consider your top competitor? Why?

____

____

____

Are they a possible strategic partner? Why or why not?

____

____

____

5. **Charities**: Community service is always a great way to connect. Giving back to the world is, simply put, *the right thing to do*.

a. When is the last time you volunteered your services or held a company-wide sponsored event that you supported not just monetarily but where you gave of your time or the time of your employees?

____

____

____

b. What is your commitment moving forward?

____

____

____

6. **Socialization:** Connecting to those around us through meaningful relationships is human nature. Whether we are deemed introverts or extroverts, we all still enjoy being around a group of peers, just talking and interacting.

a. Which networking groups do you attend, simply because you like those in attendance?

____

____

Bottom line: There are lots of good reasons to network. We do it countless times throughout our day, week, month, year and life. Stay ahead of the industry curve by aligning yourself with an organization that shares your professional interests. Connect with colleagues through one of the social media channels, newsletters or blogs. Visit and/ or join your local chamber, business networking industry (BNI), peer leadership boards, community organizations such as your local Startup or Incubator, your Junior League or Rotary. You'll stay informed while keeping a pulse on important business trends and issues with your colleagues and your community.

NETWORK DOS AND DON'TS

Don't:

- × Don't go to an event to collect business cards. The name of the game isn't *collection*, it's *CONNECTION.*
- × Don't go to an event to *party,* be professional at all times. You never know who is in attendance and who you may meet for the first time.
- × Don't go to an event without your business cards.

- × Don't walk around giving everyone your business cards without real and memorable connecting conversations.
- × Don't go to an event assuming you will make a deal or sign a new contract before you leave.
- × Don't go to an event and meet others one time and expect them to refer you with only one brief introduction.
- × Don't stay in the same group all night and appear to be unapproachable or a part of a *click* group.
- × Don't become a member and then never attend events, yet expect to get business from relationships and connections you never made. Having your name in the directory or on a website isn't nearly enough to say you made an effort to connect to those participating in the group.
- × Don't just give your introduction and walk away quickly when you see someone you know.

Do

- ✓ Do have plenty of business cards on hand.
- ✓ Give business cards out to those who directly ask you for them or hand you theirs first.
- ✓ Do research the event in advance if possible, to understand who will be in attendance and if someone is going who you have been trying to meet.
- ✓ Do ask others in your circle of influence to attend with you, so each of you can introduce one another to various already established connections and relationships. If you are

naturally an introverted individual, there is comfort with familiarity.

- ✓ Do strike up conversations with those you haven't met before.
- ✓ Do place notes on the backs or fold-over edges of cards from people you need to follow up with quickly.
- ✓ Do place your cards in one pocket and those of your new contacts in another pocket to keep them separated during the event. (Yes, you will get them confused and may hand another person's card out unknowingly. It has happened and will happen.)
- ✓ Do follow up within 24 hours with any new contact you made. Drop them a line or connect with them on LinkedIn. Always mention it was nice meeting them the previous day at ___ event. Try and set up a follow-up call or meeting over coffee to further understand each other's business. How can the two of you *help* one another in the future?
- ✓ Do go into your LinkedIn contacts and see who may know someone you're trying to meet, if they are attending the same meeting or set one up via LinkedIn asking for a group lunch meeting.
- ✓ Do keep track of all your meetings and events, the expenses, the time spent and the reason you went to fully understand the ROI and those people with whom you need to build or maintain a connection.

THE CONNECTION MAP

This story recounts one of the most successful sales (connecting) techniques I am aware of to this very day:

There was a man named Tony who worked in an office, at a desk, with a phone and computer, just like most of us. His day was spent "working his rolodex." What was his title? It doesn't matter, he was an amazing connector and he knew exactly where each piece of business came from; meaning who and how. He didn't just collect business cards, he connected people. He didn't just connect people, he gave them each a reason to connect. Every reason he connected them gave instant value back to one another.

His day was spent on the phone calling his colleagues to see what was going on, how he could help them or simply to chat. When he attended events like golf tournaments, he made sure he connected those around him. He rarely, rarely talked about his own business but he always talked about others. Everyone knew Tony and knew if he was making a connection it meant something. His opinion was valued and trusted. Why? Because he was authentic and didn't have any hidden agenda to get you to buy from him or use his services, BUT you did. His approach to life and his ability to connect on a genuine level built his brand of integrity and therefore you would never dream of going to anyone else for the same type of product and service his company offered.

I learned a lot from Tony and continue to share his style and approach with others today. He truly gave and connected first and foremost before any type of selling ever occurred. He could also tell who, in turn, was authentic. He could draw you a map of how a piece of business was sold and who, how, where and when he made the connection. He knew

the "old-school" values of trade and survival and his company thrived on that ability to connect.

When he passed away, the stories at the funeral service and those written on Facebook were all about how he helped others, connected others. The stories put together read like a novel. This person knew this person because he gave a golf lesson to so and so on, who in turn knew so and so…just amazing.

ACTION IS CALLING: Review the Playbook and your connection opportunities with your colleagues and strategic alliances

1. Make a list of all of your weekly, monthly, quarterly and annual meetings AND why you attend them. Refer to the full connection reasons listed earlier in the chapter.

Network /Meeting Name	Reason

2. Make a list of those you consider to be your competitors. This includes internally and externally. This time list the reasons why you consider them a competitor.

Network /Meeting Name	Reason

3. Take the list you made in number 2 and reconsider how you could connect in a win-win manner.
    a. Example A: Internally you are working on projects together. Perhaps your colleagues are more detail-oriented than you are and you could connect because of their attention to details.
    b. Example B: You own a consulting firm and you want to bid on a large proposal and could use another expert vs. adding employees.

Perceived Competitor	Winning Connection Option

4. Take your next month's calendar of conferences and networking events. Make a list of who you want to meet and how you can introduce them to someone you know who could help them grow and prosper.

Event	Person to Meet	Way to Connect Them to Someone You Know

5. Make a list of your recent business connections and how you know them. How did you originally meet? Have you thanked the person that introduced you or repay the favor?

Person You Know	How

6. Same concept of number 5, but this time list all the business revenue transactions you have completed over the past several weeks or months. Or list those who are your regular clients and once again recall how they became your clients. Look for the patterns, the connections as to how you received the business.

Revenue	Where Did it Come From? Who Did it Come From?

After completing the checkpoints above, you should see a pattern emerge about your networking groups, your colleagues, your opportunities and those you need to thank and/or repay. You should recognize your real purposes, some lessons learned, a need to network differently and when to pivot.

Connecting is about giving. The rest comes when we give and connect authentically. Realizing where and how you gained connections, so that you in turn can give back, is simply an example of doing the right thing.

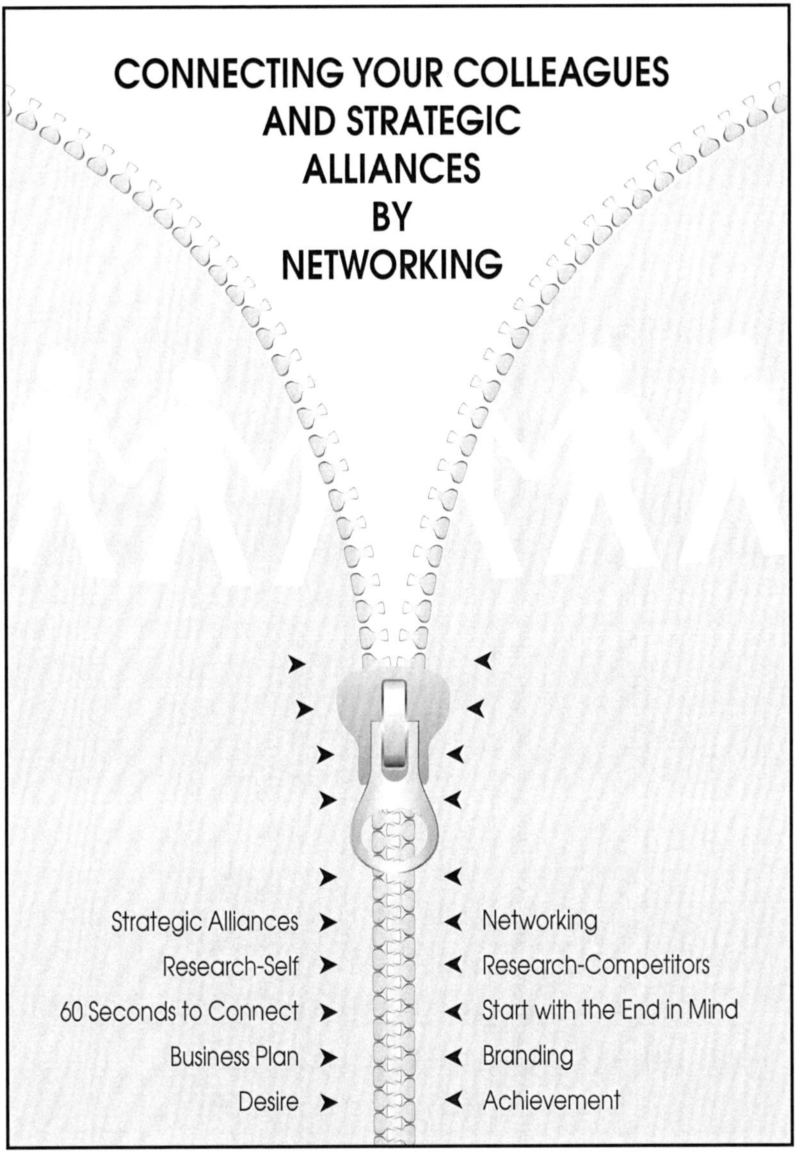

CONNECTING YOUR COLLEAGUES AND STRATEGIC ALLIANCES BY NETWORKING

Strategic Alliances ➤ ◀ Networking

Research-Self ➤ ◀ Research-Competitors

60 Seconds to Connect ➤ ◀ Start with the End in Mind

Business Plan ➤ ◀ Branding

Desire ➤ ◀ Achievement

THE ROI CONNECTION INTO GREATER PRODUCTIVE REALITIES

"Without continual growth and progress, such words as improvement, achievement, and success have no meaning."

Benjamin Franklin

CHAPTER 6

Are you looking for growth but you're not sure how to achieve it in the most productive way? Are you possibly grasping in many directions? Are you familiar with the game show from the 1970s located in Hawaii, where contestants were placed in a glass tube, like a wind tunnel, where they tried to grab money? Many times our branding, our marketing efforts are just like that whirlwind. We grasp at possibilities only to come up short when the wind is turned off. We run around trying everything without keeping track of what is and what isn't working. We just keep grabbing, trying to catch the money. Well, take heart. This chapter includes several tips on being more effective, learning exactly what is and isn't working and how you can get your best return in revenue, given your time investments.

Connecting your Data to your Metrics in a Plan with focused Actions and knowing when to Pivot will help you through your days in the whirlwind and beyond, creating Growth and a larger Return On your Investments (ROI) of time, money and overall energy. Just as the seasons change, you should revisit your information periodically to see if you need to make any pivotal adjustments.

Defining **Data** as:

1) Facts and statistics collected together for reference or analysis.

Defining **Metrics** as:

1) A method of measuring something, or the results obtained from this.

Defining **Plan** as:

1) A detailed proposal for doing or achieving something.

Defining **Action** as:

1) The fact or process of doing something, typically to achieve an established goal.

Defining **Goals** and **Objectives** as:

1) Goals and objectives describe what the program/project is striving to accomplish. Goals

depict the general programmatic outcomes, while objectives target more specific outcomes. It is common to have several objectives for each program/project goal.

Defining **Return on Investment (ROI)** as:

1) A performance measure used to evaluate the efficiency of an investment or to compare the efficiency of a number of different investments. To calculate ROI, the benefit (return) of an investment is divided by the cost of the investment; the result is expressed as a percentage or a ratio. In this case, it refers to the time you spend doing various tasks as it relates to the revenue you generate as an individual or a team.

Defining **Growth** as:

1) The process of increasing sales and profit capacity.

Defining **Pivot** as:

1) The action of turning around a point or direction.

ARE YOU READY FOR GROWTH?

With the aforementioned on your mind, let's get started with some questions and possible answers you may have. It doesn't matter if you are a one-person shop, a company in the startup phase, a long-standing company, a multi-level marketing agent or somewhere in between, you can still become more effective, focused and profitable with internal

analyses. First let's start with some questions to see if you are ready for growth.

1. QUESTION: Do you have the right team in place?

ANSWER: You know this and you have certainly heard this before but strategizing, collaborating and aligning yourself with the right amount of like-minded associates is fundamental. I used the word "associates" on purpose to allow you to encompass your employees, your peers, your colleagues, your strategic partnerships. Anyone you work with must be aligned with a common value system and "connect-ability" for growth.

YOUR ANSWER:

____

____

____

2. QUESTION: Are your customers coming to you?

ANSWER: When your business gains a certain amount of momentum in sales, profits and respect among your fellow executives within the walls of large companies, then you have a key indicator that your brand, your company, your department, your leadership is reaching a level of awareness that is positioned for increased growth and/or responsibilities.

Each additional client or strategic partner can be a catalyst for growth, even if you are initially reluctant to diversify or expand your area.

YOUR ANSWER:

____

____

____

3. QUESTION: Are you realistic about what your company can handle?

ANSWER: Understanding the particular markets you currently live in and knowing when to take on the next one plus the ability to know when to say no, to delegate or defer to others, will keep your realism in tune. Looking for and at new opportunities includes the ability to discriminate in terms of the growth you, your department and/or your company can handle. Look at your current infrastructure, resources and the economic benefits before moving forward. Ask yourself "What happens if I or we go vs. no go? Who will this affect? What is the total impact?"

YOUR ANSWER:

____

____

____

4. QUESTION: Can your personal work-life balance handle any additional workloads?

ANSWER: Are you ready, willing and able to focus and dedicate the time needed for the company growth or suggested changes? It can take up to 12 months for you and your company to get into a rhythm and routine. There is a reason why you've heard stories of rapid growth ending in the downfall of a company that couldn't keep up: Ramp up, growth and stability can take a toll on all the players. So again, make sure that on each step of the way you ask yourself, and make the connection back, who each step will affect, for how long and whether this is in alignment with the total vision, mission and overall culture.

The television show *Shark Tank* has brought many companies to rapid growth, but trying to keep up sometimes takes a bigger toll than not having sales at all.

YOUR ANSWER:

____

____

____

5. QUESTION: Do you have the cash to withstand the cycle?

ANSWER: You cannot be ready to grow unless you're in a position to carry the business until the sales catch up with the investment. Or departmentally speaking, if you haven't done the research and return in order to propose the following year's departmental budgets.

If we are talking about startups, then your forecasts must remain on the conservative side so you don't dramatically underestimate the cash flow. I have seen this happen time and time again. Everyone gets excited and their feet begin to leave the floor and they come crashing down because they had too much air in their heads to realize the true timelines to stability. Growth, continued growth and stability cost money. It is true you have to spend money to make money and anyone telling you otherwise hasn't experienced this pain and reality.

So when you think you're ready for launch or growth or increased responsibilities, make sure you have positioned yourself to carry the business or department until the sales or workforce catches up to the investment or milestones or increased funding.

As your growth and partnerships happen, make sure you connect the new systems and processes to handle the increased responsibilities and overall demand. During the growth process you need to stay connected to your core services and initial branding that generated the new opportunity. Stay connected to the WHY and your WHY every step of the way.

YOUR ANSWER:

____

____

____

6. QUESTION: Are you already meeting or exceeding your current established goals?

ANSWER: "The proof is in the pudding," is what I have always said. It's true, numbers lie if you don't know what numbers to really look for. However, if you seek results and you agreed to the final goal or outcome needed, and you meet or exceed it, then keep pushing forward to great connections and expectations. Pushing the boundaries at the right speed for the right reasons and right measures will keep your risks at bay and your fortunes in abundance.

Don't make excuses when targets are missed and don't play the pointing game either. When you can prove you can make defined objectives it builds both internal and external confidence in your ability and/or your company's ability to expand. Owning up to objectives missed is equally important in your personal branding. Remember that missed expectations add to our experience and a better understanding of what does and doesn't work.

YOUR ANSWER:

____

____

____

As an inventor, Edison made 1,000 unsuccessful attempts at inventing the light bulb. When a reporter asked, "How did it feel to fail 1,000 times?" Edison replied, "I didn't fail 1,000 times. The light bulb was an invention with 1,000 steps." Edison knew how to connect and stream together lessons into success. Do you?

YOUR DATA TRACKING, YOUR ANALYSIS AND YOUR DESIRED HOURLY BILLABLE RATES, YOUR REAL ROI CONNECTION

Now that we have reviewed and discussed whether you are ready for growth, let's break down your efforts into productive and more profitable results.

This is a common area of opportunity and understanding. When working with clients, I more often than not find they really don't know what the ROI is on each of their business segments/revenue streams. They haven't accurately calculated the time they spent on each and how much revenue was generated in the end compared to the expenses and time efforts. What they believe to be true is usually challenged when it's tracked. Knowing how and where you spend your time and your associate's time will confirm your best uses of independent time as well as the revenue you and your team generate for each activity. When you know this, you begin to make decisions based on awareness vs. assumptions. That's always a good thing.

It doesn't matter if you are a one-man shop or have thousands of employees. Growth and survival depend on your return on investment. Your investment includes your personal hourly rate. Here are some tips on figuring your time values, thus your hourly billable rate. This also allows you confidence when saying "no" to a piece of business.

Do you know how you truly spend your time? How your employees spend their time? What's effective and what could be considered a useless activity if you are trying to grow?

ACTION 1:

For at least one week, but preferably for four weeks, track and log how you spend your time and efforts in a journal or via your preferred tracking tool. (If you are a great calendar user, then go ahead and pull your past 30 days and start your breakout actions as outlined below.) Don't go overboard but use tracking by the half hour or hour. Keep track of things like:

- Admin/Office Work
    - Making and returning calls
    - Making and returning emails
    - Customer files and paperwork
    - Orders
    - Finance, AP & AR
- Networking
    - Type and include drive time to and from
- Business Development Meetings
    - Sales
        - Selling
        - Prospecting
    - Marketing
        - Idea sharing and creativity time
        - Writing content
        - Designing content

- Meetings: Board, Executive, Staff, Community
- Volunteering
- Personal Training and Development
- Executive – Employee Training and Development
- Errands
- Delegation and Follow-up
- Other

After your tracking period, place the data into an Excel spreadsheet and create some ratio pie charts. This visual will tell the story.

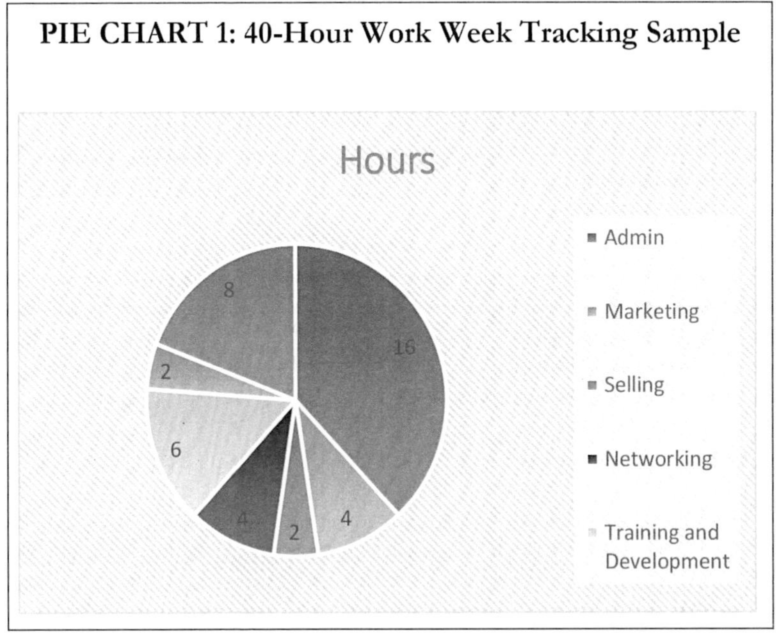

PIE CHART 1: 40-Hour Work Week Tracking Sample

ACTION 2:

Do you know what expenses were directly related to each of your time expenditures?

For the same tracking period on time, keep an accurate list of actual related expenses: gas, office supplies, meals, gifts, etc. Just as before, input your data into an Excel sheet. Once again, your visual will tell the story.

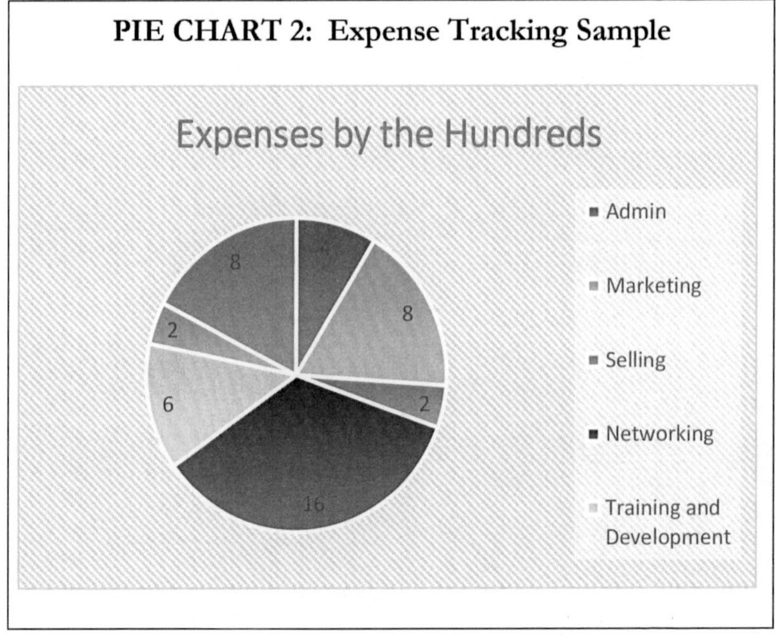

PIE CHART 2: Expense Tracking Sample

ACTION 3:

Do you know all of your revenues by your business types, segments?

Again, for the same tracking timeframe list the revenues you gained by each activity/revenue segment. Place this data into the same Excel sheet you have been working with and create your pie chart.

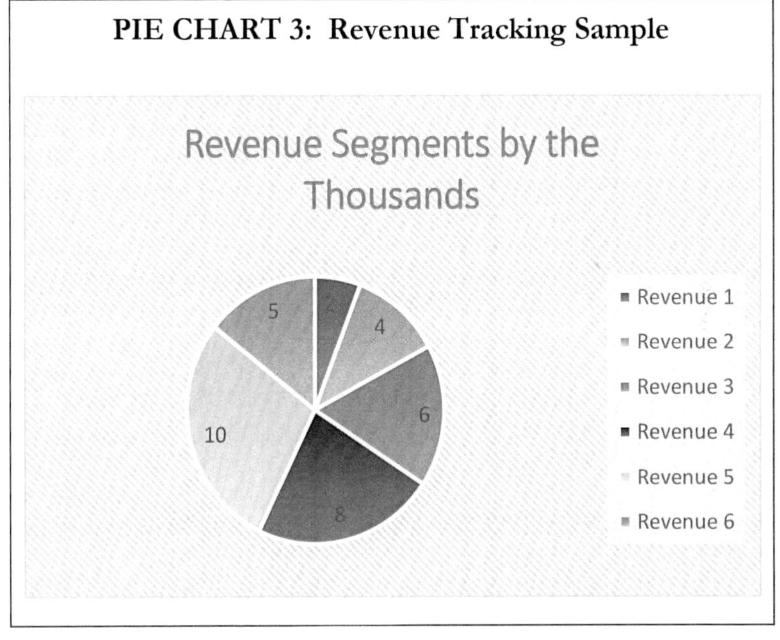

PIE CHART 3: Revenue Tracking Sample

ACTION 4:

Do you know your return on your investment by business type/segment and by the hours you spent?

Take each segment's revenue divided by the expenses and then divided by the hours spent. This shows you the exact return and your true hourly billing rate. Then ask yourself if these ratios are what you expected and need.

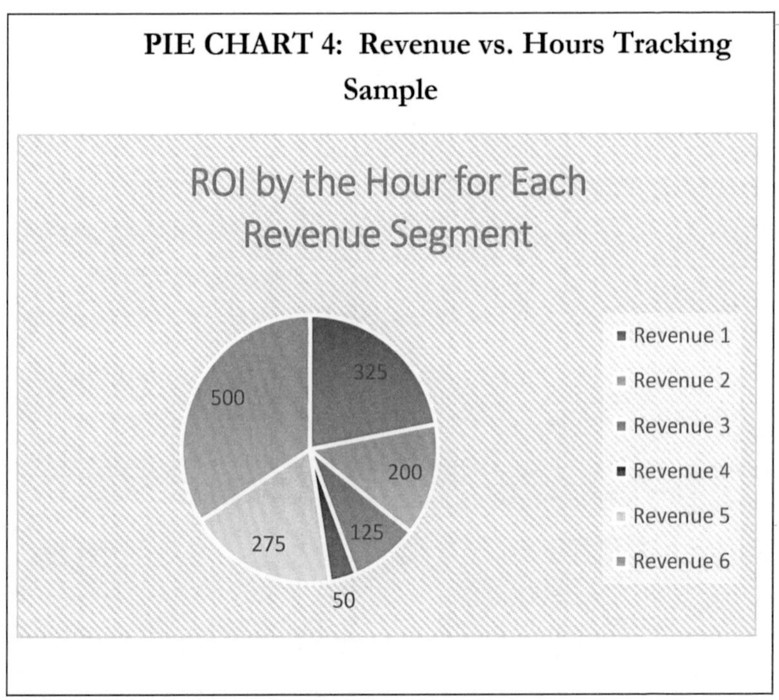

PIE CHART 4: Revenue vs. Hours Tracking Sample

Now that you have this information, you can update occasionally and certainly adjust your time spent, and make

time management, hiring, marketing decisions and much more based on black and white numbers vs. instincts and assumptions.

One of the enlightening moments for most business developers, owners and executives is the amount of time spent doing administrative work. That time is better spent building the business, working on the business instead of in the business. **Bottom line:** You will realize the need to outsource some items. Common items include payroll, bookkeeping, human resources and marketing such as research, ads, website, social media and more.

One such business owner found his average billable hours by revenue segment ranging from $539 an hour to $256 an hour but he spent 40% of his time doing administrative work. All he had to do was hire a $15 an hour office coordinator for eight hours a week, reducing his administrative work to 20% of his time and increasing his monthly revenue by $12,800. His expenses increased by $624 but with a net revenue increase of $12,176 in just one month. That's a no-brainer but if he didn't stop to track, analyze and realize the connection between shifting his work load to the right person so he could bring in more business, he would still be spending his time doing things that don't allow him to grow, working **on** the business instead of **in** the business.

The second biggest consistent surprise owners discover is the time spent on each revenue segment or stream you have in your business and the amount made by the hour for those efforts. This can help justify your billable fees for services and products with increases in pricing or increase in focus by segment or volume. For those of you doing pro bono work, it can help to increase your confidence in what to charge and when to charge for consulting fees, for example. Many business owners and executives find huge opportunities to pivot during these types of data collection and analysis. Remember, it's not the metrics you track, it's what you do with the information and how you turn the discoveries into new goals and objectives that make your business grow.

The business owner who did a lot of pro-bono work needed to build his confidence when doing annual reviews with his clients' portfolios. He realized how much he was diluting his hourly rate and believed that if he just increased his volume on reviews he could validate a lower cost point, which was higher than always doing the work for free. He still does some gratis work but not as often. In his case, when he billed anything below his lowest average billable rate of $256, he was making a conscious decision vs. being unaware of his big-picture revenue decisions.

As you move into this chapter's Playbook action review, keep in mind you can do these activities for each portion of your business no matter how big or small your employee count. These activities are great for full-time

workers with outside revenue streams, those in home businesses or in multi-level marketing firms, ensuring that your hours spent and the expenses associated with them are given back in the revenue needed to sustain the business and your long-term sanity. The same can be applied to volunteer groups you are associated with as well. This chapter's review takes you back to the chapter's beginning with goals and objectives, but don't forget the lessons learned from your pie charts as you complete this review and set new objectives and involvement from others.

ACTION IS CALLING: Connecting Your Objectives and Growth with the Right Timing

Think of a time you missed an objective.

1. What was it?

   ____

   ____

   ____

2. Who was involved? Why?

   ____

   ____

   ____

3. What was your action plan?

   ____

   ____

   ____

4. How did you determine the milestones?

____

____

____

5. How did you connect the process; convert the words into action?

____

____

____

6. How frequently did you stop, reflect and pivot? And why?

____

____

7. What did your data say?

____

____

____

8. What metrics were used? And why?

____

____

____

9. What worked? Why?

____

____

____

10. What didn't? Why?

____

____

____

11. What did you learn?

____

____

____

12. What was the final outcome, cause and effect?

____

____

____

13. Did you pivot? Why or why not?

____

____

____

14. Do you view this reasoning and outcome differently now? Why or why not?

____

____

____

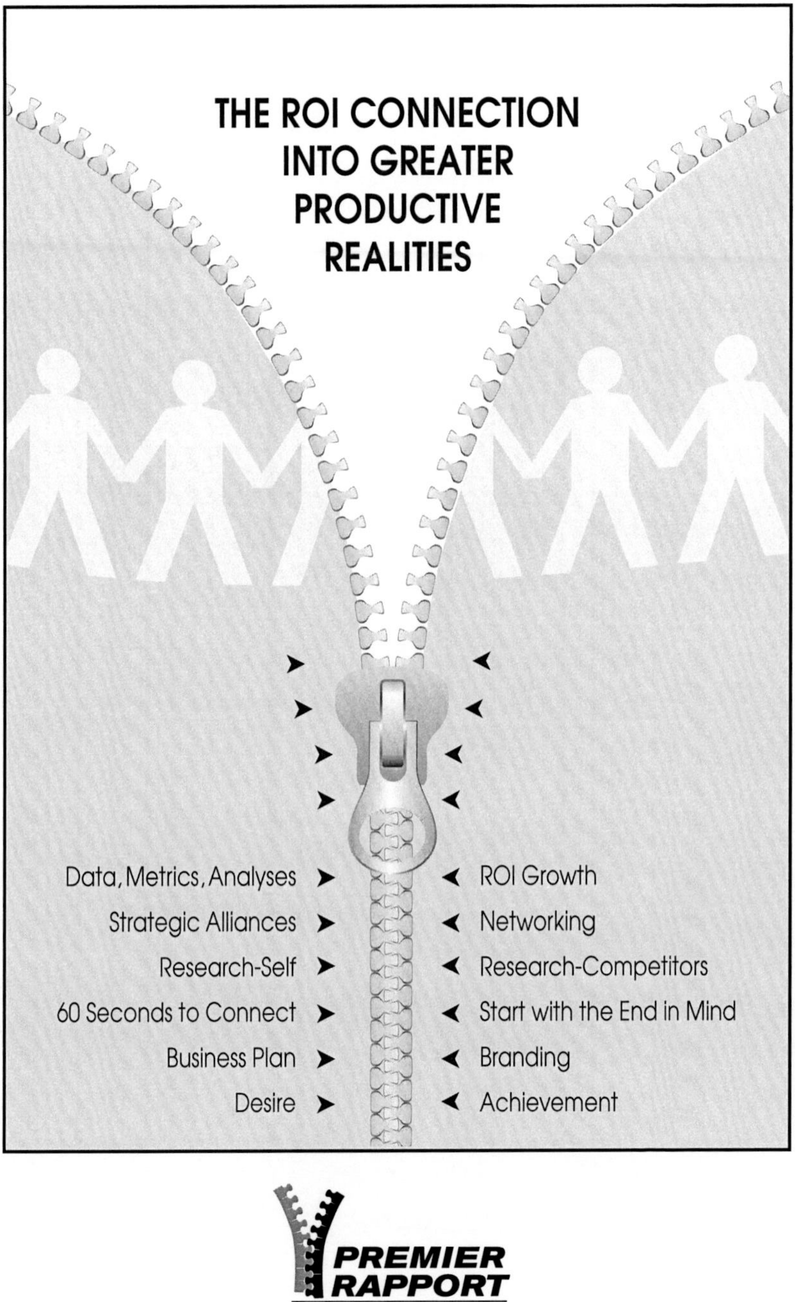

THE ROI CONNECTION INTO GREATER PRODUCTIVE REALITIES

Data, Metrics, Analyses ➤	◀ ROI Growth
Strategic Alliances ➤	◀ Networking
Research-Self ➤	◀ Research-Competitors
60 Seconds to Connect ➤	◀ Start with the End in Mind
Business Plan ➤	◀ Branding
Desire ➤	◀ Achievement

CONNECTING YOUR PRESENT TO YOUR FUTURE VIA SUCCESSION PLANNING

"Most business owners spend more time planning their next vacation than they do planning for their retirement for their business."

Doug Robbins

CHAPTER 7

When the subject of succession planning comes up in a conversation, I am never sure where the discussion will lead. Why? Because succession planning has several meanings and interpretations depending on the size of the company or the individual you are talking to. In this chapter, we will discuss all the facets of this topic and how the proper connections will keep you and your company on point.

Those of you who have gone in front of a venture capitalist or an investor, already know that they ask you about your exit strategy as a part of your startup planning. Have you ever asked yourself what would happen if you became incapacitated, unable to run your company or your department? Who would take over? What would happen to you, your company and your family? Succession planning isn't one thing, its many things, including developing those around you to step up long after you are gone or when a tragedy strikes.

Defining **Talent Management** as:

1) Talent management is the integrated process of ensuring that an organization has a continuous supply of highly productive individuals in the right job at the right time.

Defining **Talent Replacement** as:

1) A system related to succession planning is the identification of emergency step-in candidates or talent replacement. It is often useful to identify not only a permanent replacement, but also candidates who can keep things going temporarily. These include individuals capable of performing the basic, short-term tasks of critical positions until the return of the incumbent or the appointment of a qualified candidate.

Defining **Succession Planning** as:

1) A process for identifying and developing internal people with the potential to fill key business leadership positions in the company.

Defining **Exit Strategy** as:

1) The process of explicitly defining exit-related objectives for the owner(s) of a business, followed by the design of a comprehensive strategy and road map that take into account all personal, business, financial, legal and taxation aspects of achieving those objectives, usually in the context of planning the leadership succession and continuity of a business.

Defining **Organizational Development** as:

1) A deliberately planned, organization-wide effort to increase an organization's effectiveness and/or efficiency so as to enable the organization to achieve its strategic goals.

Defining **Core Competency** as:

1) The main strengths or strategic advantages of a business. Core competencies are the combination of pooled knowledge and technical capacities that allow a business to be competitive in the marketplace. Theoretically, a core competency should allow a company to expand into new end markets as well as provide a significant benefit to customers. It should also be hard for competitors to replicate.

Defining **Behavioral Assessment** as:

1) An approach to understanding and changing behavior by identifying the context in which it occurs (the situations or stimuli that either precede or follow it). It involves recording the frequency of various behaviors, an approach that focuses on the interactions between situations and behaviors for the purpose of effecting behavioral change.

As we dive into succession planning, let's first set the stage with some questions.

- Do you have a plan? If yes, is it clear and are you focused?
- Do you understand the overall need for a plan?
- Do you realize it keeps you connected to the bigger picture?

Again, it doesn't matter if you are an individual or a large corporation, succession planning is fundamental for your future.

ADVANTAGES OF SUCCESSION PLANNING

Both employees and the business benefit from long-term succession planning regardless of which form it takes. On the employee side, a formal succession plan tells employees that the business values and is committed to its staff. Advancement opportunities often increase morale and employee engagement, causing a corresponding decrease in employee

turnover rates. On the employer side, succession planning supports continuity and sustainability objectives, ensuring the business is capable of moving forward whether key staff members leave voluntarily, due to retirement or via termination proceedings. As already discussed, there are many types of succession planning. What are you planning and do you have the following covered?

- Formal Succession Plan and Company Exit
- Designated Replacement in case of emergency
- Target Date Replacement – for retirement
- Talent Development
- Job Replacement
- Situational Replacement – specific roles
- Growth Replacement

EXIT STRATEGY PLANNING STEPS AND POSSIBLE IDEAS

Step 1

Find and train the right person to fill your shoes if you decide upon the first level of succession planning. Allow enough time to train your successor so he can make the leap from employee to owner. Let your successor watch and learn what you do daily to run the business. Allow your successor to progressively take over your ownership duties and responsibilities. Make sure he understands the business' philosophy and long-term goals. Keep your employees informed of the ownership changes so your daily operations do not suffer.

Step 2

Transfer ownership to the next owner. This is the second level of succession planning. Take the sale proceeds and use them to fund your retirement if you are selling your business to employees or people outside of the business. If your children are taking over, you can sell the business to them and distribute the proceeds to your children after meeting your retirement needs. If you have already funded your retirement, you can gift the business to the children who are actively involved with the daily operation. Gift an equal dollar value of non-business assets to the children not involved with your business to prevent hurt feelings.

Step 3

Sell or gift your business if you prefer to act on the third level of succession planning. Gifting the business lets you use the federal gift tax exemption to lower the transfer tax liability. At the time of publication, you can give a $14,000 tax-free gift to an individual for each tax year. If your spouse is a co-seller, the two of you can give a combined tax-free gift of $28,000. For example, if your business is worth $100,000 and you have four children, you can gift each one $28,000 and bring the transfer tax down to zero. Contact an estate- planning attorney to structure the sale to minimize your tax liability.

Check Point

1. Do any of these fit you? What are some immediate thoughts you want to capture?
   a. Right Person?

      ____

   b. Transfer Ownership?

      ____

   c. Gift?

      ____

TALENT DEVELOPMENT

Foundation and Workforce Strength

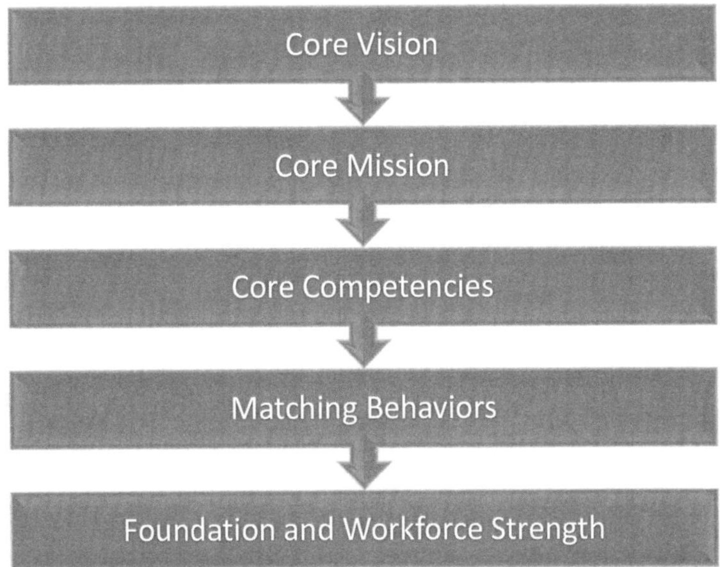

Please notice in Figure 1, I used the word "development" and not "management." We aren't trying to hold people down, but rather lift them up with intentional, laser-focused strategies, goals and objectives. It's big-picture thinking with the ability to pivot as necessary.

- Core Vision and Mission
  - Check back in your notes from Chapter 2
- Core Competencies

  A business just starting out will try to first identify, and then focus on its core competencies, allowing it to establish a footprint while gaining a solid reputation and brand recognition. Using, and later leveraging, core competencies usually provides the best chance for a company's continued growth and survival, as these factors are what differentiate the company from competitors.

  An example from a well-established company: Founded in 1892, B. F. Saul Company has been one of the most successful privately-owned real estate companies in the United States. Their growth has been the result of a commitment to exacting standards and the belief that knowledge of the marketplace, when paired with the ability to commit substantial resources, will bring exceptional rewards. Their company's core competencies include Ethics, Results and Vision.

  - Ask yourself what are the core competencies in your department, your company? Should they

be changed or modified? Are they in complete alignment with your Vision and Mission?

____

____

____

- Matching Behaviors using an assessment tool

Using behavioral assessment tools gives you the quick heads up by knowing what drives and motivates not only you but, more importantly, those around you. One such great tool is Predictive Index®. *1

The Predictive Index (PI®) is a theory-based, self-report measurement of normal, adult, work-related personality that has been developed and validated for use within occupational and organizational populations.

The PI is used for a variety of personnel management purposes, including employee selection, executive on-boarding, leadership development, succession planning, performance coaching, team-building and organizational culture change, among others.

The assessment is un-timed, generally takes approximately five to ten minutes to complete, and is available in paper-and-pencil, desktop, Web-based formats and mobile devices.

The PI measures four primary and fundamental personality constructs:

1. Dominance: The degree to which an individual seeks to control his or her environment. Individuals who score high on this dimension are independent, assertive and self-confident. Individuals who score low on this dimension are agreeable, cooperative and accommodating.

2. Extroversion: The degree to which an individual seeks social interaction with other people. Individuals who score high on this dimension are outgoing, persuasive and socially poised. Individuals who score low on this dimension are serious, introspective and task-oriented.

3. Patience: The degree to which an individual seeks consistency and stability in his or her environment. Individuals who score high on this dimension are patient, consistent and deliberate. Individuals who score low on this dimension are fast-paced, urgent and intense.

4. Formality: The degree to which an individual seeks to conform to formal rules and structure. Individuals who score high on this dimension are organized, precise and self-disciplined. Individuals who score low on this dimension are informal, casual and uninhibited.

*For more information on Predictive Index you can visit www.piworldwide.com or www.pimidlantic.com.

When these steps are properly connected, they provide you with a strong roadmap and with clarity for workforce planning for the long haul.

Check Point

What behavioral strengths do you look for? Are the executives in your team leading with those strengths and motivating others? Do your job descriptions, job ads and performance development systems all match in complete alignment? In Chapter 8, Elizabeth Veliz, with Adelante HR Consulting, discusses "employee engagement." So we will take a deeper dive into that full connection. Until then, please take a moment and capture your thoughts here so you can reflect back.

____

____

____

____

____

____

____

____

____

____

In Figure 2, we summarize another way to connect to "Succession Planning and Talent Development:" Old Way vs. New Way

	Old Way	New Way
Talent Mindset	Having good people is one of many important performance levers. HR is responsible for people management including recruiting, compensation, performance reviews and succession planning.	Having the right talent throughout the organization is a critical source of competitive advantage. Every manager – starting with the CEO – is responsible for attracting, developing, exciting, and retaining talented people; indeed, every manager is explicitly accountable for the strength of the talent pool he/she builds.
Employee Value Proposition	We expect people to pay their dues and work their way up the line before they get the top jobs and big bucks. We have a strong value proposition that attracts customers.	We think of our people as volunteers and know we have to try to deliver on their dreams now if we are to keep them. We also have a distinctive employee value proposition that attracts and retains talented people.
Recruiting	Recruiting is like purchasing: it's about picking the best from a long line of candidates. We hire at entry levels only, primarily from the same schools.	Recruiting is more like marketing and selling; it's a key responsibility of all managers. We hire at all levels – entry, mid, and top – and look for talent in every conceivable field.
Growing Leaders	Development is training. Development happens when you are fortunate enough to get a really good boss.	Development happens through a series of challenging job experiences and candid, helpful coaching. Development is crucial to performance and retention…and it can be institutionalized.
Differentiation	Differentiation undermines teamwork.	We shower our top performers with opportunities and recognition. We develop and nurture mid-performers. We help our lower performers raise their game or we move them out or aside.

FULL CONNECTION AND ENGAGEMENT

The next three figures provide the connections points for higher returns and longevity. They are intended to be self-explanatory. Starting with:

- ✓ Why we do what we do?
- ✓ How do we accomplish this?
- ✓ What are our results when we connect all three together?

Again, Chapters 7 and 8 are strongly connected to the interworking of a company, a department and all teams. Collaborating and connecting together always yields higher returns for everyone involved.

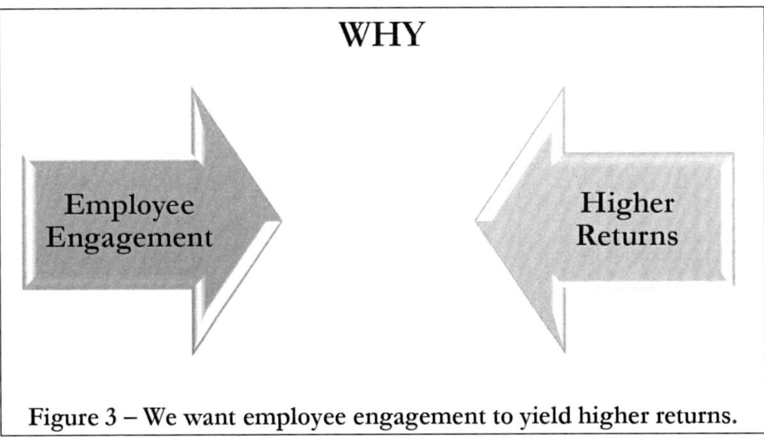

Figure 3 – We want employee engagement to yield higher returns.

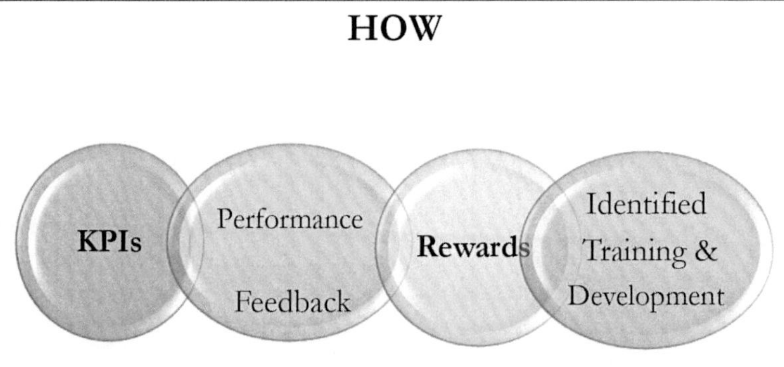

Figure 4 – Connecting performance indicators with ongoing feedback, including rewards, helps you to continually identify the training and development needs for individuals and teams.

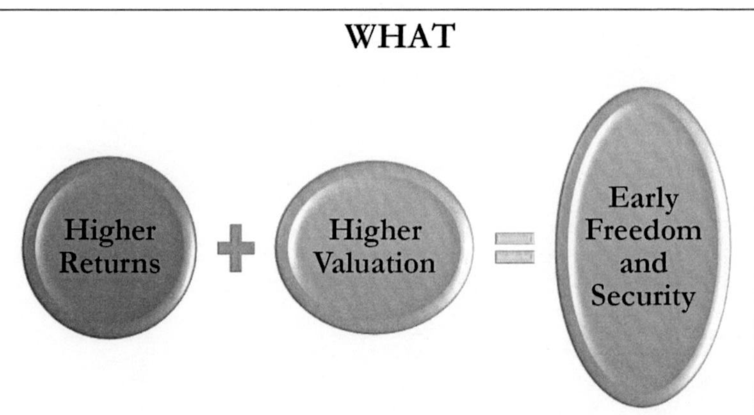

Figure 5 – Finally, with higher returns from your efforts in Figure 4, you achieve a higher valuation for your company, which leads to earlier exit planning and financial freedom.

ACTION IS CALLING: Your Succession Planning Readiness Checklist *2

Planning emotionally to exit from your business

1) Have you decided when you would prefer to exit your business?
2) How excited are you about operating your business each day?
3) Have you considered how you will spend your time when you leave the business?
4) Do you have a clear idea of what exactly is being sold? For example, are you selling your clients, business contracts, equipment, business systems with intellectual property, business premises, business license such as fishing license, income revenue, etc.?
5) How realistic is your timeline in deciding the period of time to exit your business? What makes you think you are realistic about this expectation?
6) How likely is it that your business would thrive in the hands of a more vibrant leader?
7) Have you considered the effect on the business if you continue to stay too long?
8) If closing down is the only option you can consider, what advice have you sought about this? Is it possible there may be things you could do to ensure your business could be sold?

Planning for contingencies

1) Do you have a formal plan to cover exiting your business if you are forced to leave due to illness, accident, partner dispute, and sudden loss of license, death or other mishap? If so, what are the details?

2) Would you want the ability to be able to buy out your business partners if they suddenly departed from the business rather than work with their chosen successors or beneficiaries?

Communicating your succession plan

1) Have you communicated your plans to parties of concern, such as your family, business partners, key staff, etc.?
2) Have you considered how communicating your intended exit may impact upon your business when clients, staff and/or suppliers learn of your plans? How will you deal with this? What can you do to alleviate any unintended impact?
3) If you have communicated your plans, how have you done this and what response did you receive?
4) If you have not communicated your plans, how and when do you plan to do this?

Business valuation

1) Are you relying on the sale of your business to fund the next phase of your life, and if so, how much will you need for this purpose?
2) What measures have you taken to properly value your business at the current time?
3) If you have had your business professionally valued, are you happy with the business valuation you have obtained? If not, what will you do to improve the value of your business?
4) What have you learned or discovered from the sale and valuation of your competitors' businesses that will assist you in determining the value of your type of business?

5) Are there any factors about your business that will enhance or impair your business valuation? If so, what are these and how are you going to change your business to ensure this problem is eliminated?

Identifying candidates to succeed you

1) Who have you identified as a possible candidate to take over your business?
2) What action have you taken to ensure the candidates identified will be willing and in the financial position to buy your business ownership?
3) If you are intending to sell on the open market, have you considered prevailing market conditions to make certain this will be possible?
4) Have you identified the most likely sources of buyers for your business, and if so, who and how will you target them to sell your business?
5) Is it possible that a merger with a competitor is the most likely scenario for a successful business exit?
6) Have you considered an employee shareholder arrangement to organize a buyout over time?

Passing the business to family

1) Have you chosen the most suitable family member to whom to pass your business, based on qualifications, skill, passion, willingness and capabilities? Or have you decided by marriage, sex, birthright or your wishes alone?
2) How well prepared to run your business is the person you are intending to hand the business over to?
3) Have you considered how the remaining siblings in the business will view your choice of new leader? Are they likely to support your decision?

4) Have you worked out how you can make the financial arrangements of the handover fair to all siblings, including those who will not be involved in the business as an ongoing concern?
5) Are you ready to relinquish power to your chosen successor, or are you still going to retain control of the main decisions within the business? If so, how is this likely to impact the morale and satisfaction of the new business leader?
6) Have you considered setting up a board of non-family members to provide impartial assessment and/or business management of operations to alleviate family arguments?
7) What options will you consider for selling your business if none of the family members wish to assume control?

Business operations

1) Is your business ready to sell today? If so, what makes you certain your business is an attractive option for potential buyers over and above other similar businesses?
2) Are your business operations systemized with written manuals?
3) Do you have written job descriptions and training procedures manuals for all staff positions including your own? If not, how do new staff members learn their jobs?
4) How clearly can you identify your customer base and suppliers? What mechanisms do you have in place for this purpose?
5) Do you have documented contracts with your clients? If not, how can you be assured of ongoing revenue from them?

6) What lead generation systems do you have in place that will demonstrate to buyers that your business is offering potential for growth?
7) How have you handled changes in technology and product or service updates to ensure your business has a viable future as an ongoing concern?
8) If you or another business structure of yours owns the business premises where your business operates, what are your plans for that property? Is it to be leased back to the new owners or will it be sold with the business or as a separate proposition?
9) How well have you accounted for the business assets?
10) How up to date is your list of customers who owe money to you?
11) Have you made provisions for staff for long service leave, holiday pay and superannuation? If so, how have you arranged this?
12) Have you arranged a stock-take for an intended sale, and if so, how will you want to handle adjustments in the sale of your business?

<u>Business succession readiness–taxation</u>

1) What do you understand about the tax implications of selling or leaving your business, and how will you deal with this?
2) If you are exiting your business unexpectedly due to health problems, are you aware of the tax implications that may apply to any insurance proceeds you or your business partners may receive? And if so, how will you alleviate this tax?
3) What are the tax implications of an employee share arrangement for organizing a succession plan?

4) What options are you prepared to consider to assist you in managing taxation?

Business succession readiness–business broker

1) Are you prepared for the due diligence process a potential buyer will want to put you through to see if your business is one they would want to buy? What arrangements have you made to assist with this process?
2) Have you thought about the sale price at which you will list your business? How have you established a reasonable basis for setting this price?
3) Are there any special requirements of a new owner that limit who you may sell to, such as qualifications, licensing requirements or training standards to attain?
4) What sale terms would you like to include in a settlement; e.g., covenants, confidentiality agreement, warranty offers, expectations for settlement, payment terms, etc.?

Business succession readiness–financial advice

1) What are the options for dealing with sale proceeds; e.g., rolling over, purchasing another business?
2) Who will coordinate your succession plan process?
3) Where will you obtain all the relevant information for the options available to you in organizing the most suitable succession plan?
4) If you have a buy/sell arrangement, does it take into consideration contingencies such as disputes, divorce and unexpected or sudden events?

5) If you have a buy/sell arrangement, does it take into consideration business guarantees and debt arrangement between the partners or co-owners?
6) If you have a buy/sell arrangement, is it structured in a favorable way to deal with taxation issues?
7) If you have a buy/sell arrangement, does it take into consideration an exit structure for partners or co-owners to retire with their full financial entitlements?
8) If you have a buy/sell arrangement, how flexible is it to allow for changing circumstance of the business without having to re-arrange expensive new legal agreements?
9) If selling to an external party, do the sales terms provide a covenant on you not to compete within a certain time-frame or territory?
10) If selling to an external party, do the sales terms include a management consultancy requirement of you for a period of time to assist in the handover of the business?
11) Have any agreements been made for a formal succession plan with terms acceptable to each relevant party?

Sources:

1) Predictive Index® (PI®) – www.piworldwide.com and www.pimidlantic.com
2) Leigh Riley, *Good with Your Business Succession – GWYBS* – www.YourBusinessSuccession.com

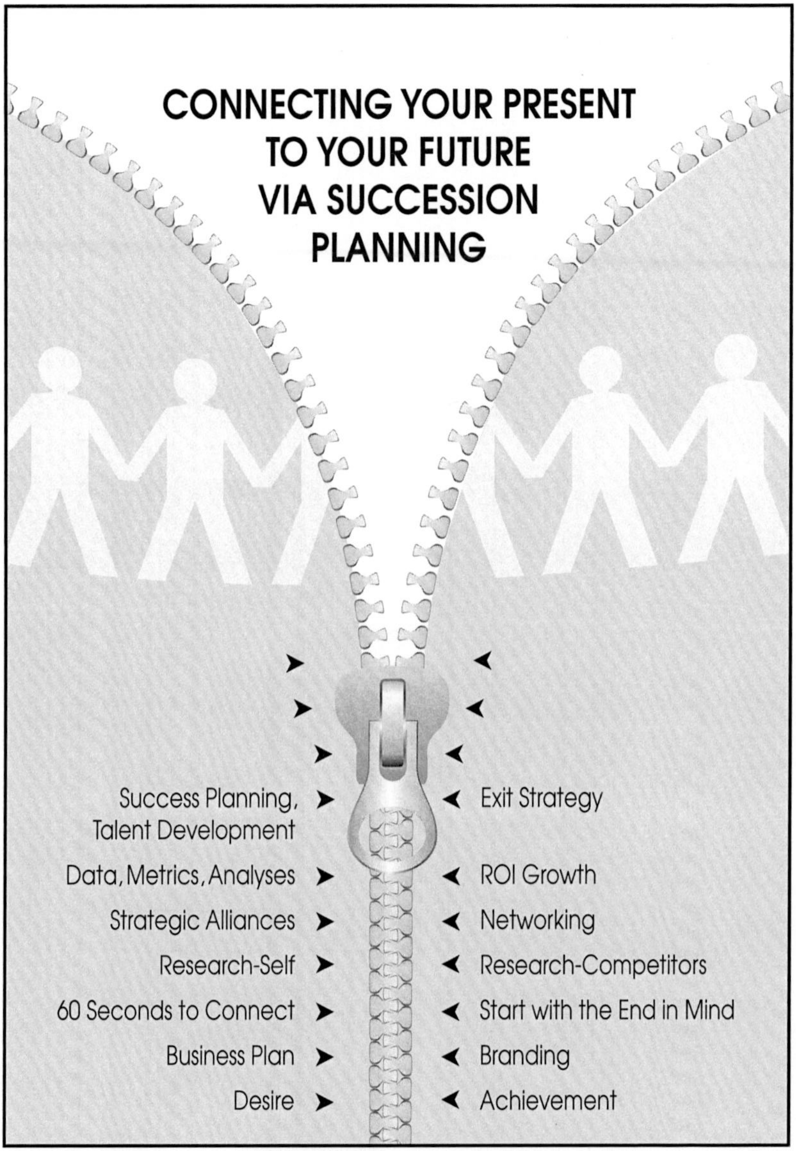

CONNECTING YOUR PRESENT TO YOUR FUTURE VIA SUCCESSION PLANNING

Success Planning, Talent Development ➤	➤ Exit Strategy
Data, Metrics, Analyses ➤	➤ ROI Growth
Strategic Alliances ➤	➤ Networking
Research-Self ➤	➤ Research-Competitors
60 Seconds to Connect ➤	➤ Start with the End in Mind
Business Plan ➤	➤ Branding
Desire ➤	➤ Achievement

THE TRUST, DELEGATION AND ACCOUNTABILITY CONNECTION TO FREEDOM

"When your teammate looks you in the eye and holds you accountable, that's the greatest kind of leadership there is."

Doug Collins

CHAPTER 8

Delegation and Accountability shouldn't be words that add "stress" in your world, but instead should give you a sense of freedom, accomplishment and ability to provide growth to those around you, leading to greater connections in trust, production, focus and profits.

Defining **Trust** as:

1) Reliance on the integrity, strength, ability, surety, etc., of a person or thing; confidence.

2) Confident expectations of something; hope.

3) The condition of one to whom something has been entrusted.

Defining **Accountability** as:

1) Subject to the obligation to report, explain, or justify something; responsible.

2) Capable of being explained; explicable; explainable.

Defining **Delegation** as:

1) To send or appoint (a person) to a duty, project or task.

2) To commit (powers, functions, etc.) to another person.

Defining **Freedom** as:

1) Exemption from external control, interference, regulation, etc.

2) The power to determine action without restraint.

ACCOUNTABILITY AND THE DEEP PURPLE CHAIR

Here's the story about the Deep Purple Chair.

There was a CEO with a deep purple chair. The story begins with a newly hired human resources director attending her first executive staff meeting. As she entered the large office held by the CEO, she noticed several chairs, one of which was a deep purple color, her favorite color, so she decided to sit in the chair. Something interesting happened as soon as she sat down—the other executives in the room, almost in unison, said, "Oooohhhh, you sat in the deep purple chair," in a concerned tone. The new director quickly inquired about the chair and found out it was the "accountability chair." When you didn't do something the CEO expected, she would bring you into the office, and somehow the deep purple chair is where you would always end up sitting. Employees described the CEO as firm and fair with high expectations. When those expectations were missed and you let her and/or the team down, she would bring you in to "talk" about what happened–to hold you accountable. However, she never made you feel less than a real person or strung on a post for a lashing. Instead she lifted you up and helped you see the honor in meeting the expectations. She was a multiplier vs. a destroyer. The Deep Purple Chair was highly regarded as well as the CEO who founded it.

Accountability is an important leadership skill to keep you and your staff connected. **Does your organization have a Deep Purple Chair in it?**

CONNECTING TRUST, DELEGATION, ACCOUNTABILITY AND FREEDOM

When we first trust, we secure the conversations that allow us to delegate to those with the ability and passions to complete the task. When we delegate to those we trust, we are naturally more comfortable holding them accountable. When those elements of trust, delegation and accountability connect, all parties enjoy freedom and comfort.

1. Trust can start by encouraging your employees and colleagues to disagree with you. Companies and individuals get into trouble when everyone is afraid to speak the truth to those in perceived power. If all you hear is how great you're doing, that should be a danger sign. Asking for open dialogue without your human defensive system coming into play on a continual basis keeps the door open.

2. Don't "micromanage," another word we all seem to dislike. Micromanaging gives the impression that you don't trust others to do the job. When you hire right, connect right and match skills and natural behaviors right, you should be able to trust, delegate and follow up (accountability) with ease and comfort. You shouldn't feel as though you have to micromanage.

And you certainly don't want to be viewed and described as a micromanager.

3. Trust is also formed by our communication about, and reactions to, various situations. When people err, don't destroy them, but make sure they learn the lessons their mistakes can teach. Connect the dots for all parties involved and make it an experience gained through conversation and reflection.

4. Accountability is being firm and fair. The ability to show compassion. Again, it involves the ability to develop strong interpersonal relationships at work, so employees have some meaning attached to the work they are doing. Accountability connects the individuals to the team and the team to the bigger goal and vision. These types of connections enhance the overall engagement, organically.

5. Connect your own learnings and curiosities by taking risks and asking yourself, "What is it that I don't know that I should know? How do I learn it and test in out in situations that are not necessarily safe?"

6. Have the ability to know yourself, but more so the ability to set yourself aside and connect to the motivational needs of those around you.

7. Be laser-focused and stick to one goal at a time. As leaders, as owners, we often choose too many development goals. Give yourself and your team the greatest chance for victory by developing one thing at a time. Celebrate the success of *each* victory along the way, no matter how small, connecting why success was achieved. Lots of little successes build into long-term, long-lasting business success, just as it is in your personal life. For example, it's the ongoing support and attention you give your children over and over again that makes them strong, healthy and responsible adults.

8. You have heard me say this repeatedly: Match the right behaviors to the right jobs, the right teams and the right culture. Don't force-fit people into organizational charts; fit organizational charts to your vision and mission and then define the required competencies, matching behaviors to the right people. It's not about getting rid of poor managers; maybe you put them in the wrong circumstance to begin with. Double check your expectations first and then realign. Everyone wins with a slow-to-hire approach, making the right connections.

9. Reflect, reevaluate and make the necessary pivots daily to ensure you have or are continually building trust. This allows for a comfortable passing of the ball

(delegation) and smooth follow up (accountability), creating success and strength (freedom).

ACTION IS CALLING: Review the Playbook and your ability to build Trust, to Delegate and to hold yourself and others Accountable.

Trust

1. Have you ever disclosed to others your perceived weaknesses?
2. Do you own your mistakes?
3. Do you shout the successes of others from the roof tops, or do you take credit for their ideas?
4. Do you offer to help others outside of your own responsibilities?
5. Do you listen before jumping to conclusions? Ask questions to seek clarity?
6. Do you fail to recognize others' skills and tap into their experiences?
7. Do you dread meetings and try and find reasons not to attend?

If you answered yes to any of these questions, take some time to make an action plan. Making the commitment to yourself first and then sharing your plans with others will more than likely make them come true. Asking others to help you and holding yourself accountable automatically builds trust and deepens the relationship connection.

____

____

____

<u>Delegation</u>

1. Do you *own* everything about your position, never asking others for help? Even single department managers and sole proprietors need to answer this question.
2. Do you truly know your own strengths, skill sets, experience and passions and those of the people around you? Do you tap into them?
3. Do you seek clarity and understanding to ensure you are on the same page when asking others to complete a job, a task, a project? Did they describe the expectation back to you as you had envisioned it and in the timeline you had in your head? Did you ask?
4. Did you ask yourself whether you are the right person to be doing the task on your to-do list? Is there someone else better suited? What is the cost to me, my career, and my company if I keep the *task* or delegate it to the *right* person?

Again, if you answered yes to any of these questions, take some time to make an action plan. What is stopping me from delegating those things that I really shouldn't be doing? What can I do differently? Who can I start with to assist? What is on my to-do list, and if I don't do it, what will happen? Who will that affect?

____

____

____

____

Accountability

1. When setting deadlines with others, do you ask them to set the timeframe? Or do you:
    a. Self-set
    b. Other-set
    c. Collaboratively-set
2. Is everyone on your team measured to the same standards of performance and overall expectations? Would everyone on your team agree with your answer? Why or why not?

    ____

    ____

    ____

3. Does the average day for you and those around you include accountability with check-ins and check-ups via comfortable conversations? Are you perceived as a micromanager? What is your communication approach, telling or selling?
4. Do you share your goals and action items so others can hold you accountable as well?

    ____

    ____

    ____

    ____

Freedom

1. How would you describe your freedom at work?

2. How would those around you describe theirs?

It is true, freedom does take time, energy and sometimes pain, but WOW is it worth it! The rewards to making the Freedom Connection are endless. Give it a try, one *Connection* at a time.

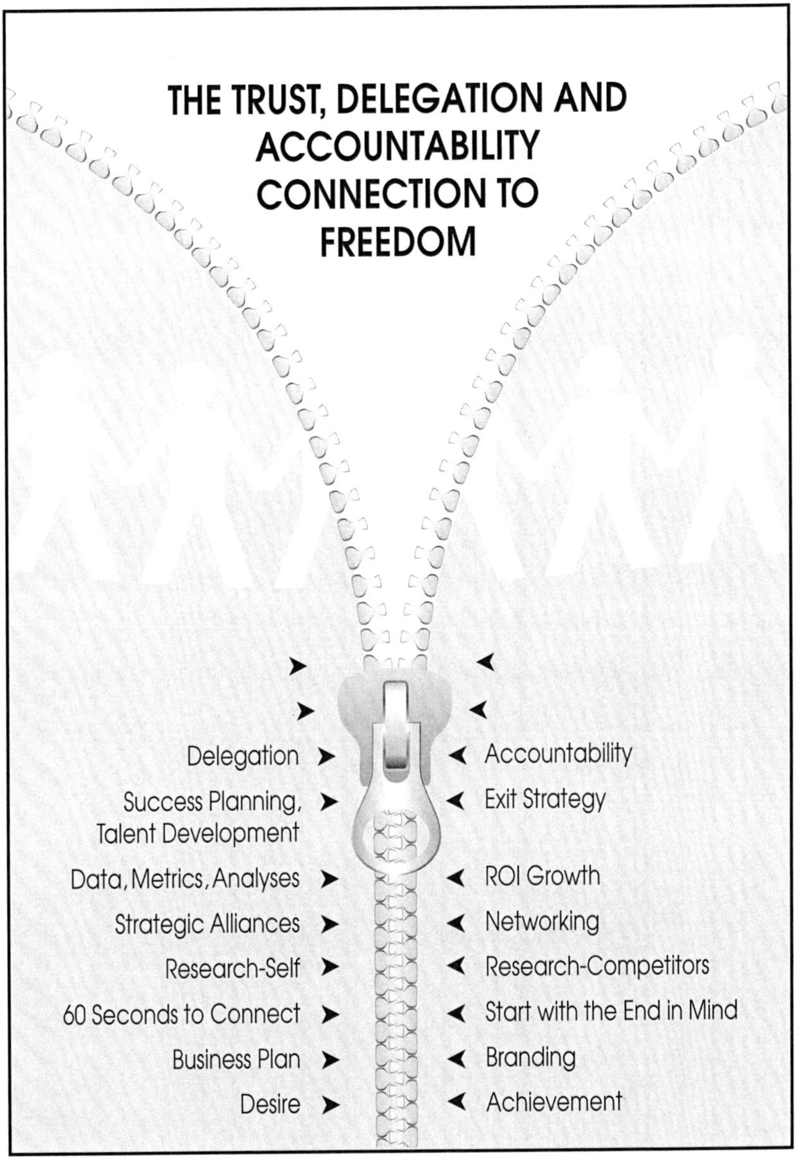

THE TRUST, DELEGATION AND ACCOUNTABILITY CONNECTION TO FREEDOM

Delegation ➤	➤ Accountability
Success Planning, Talent Development ➤	➤ Exit Strategy
Data, Metrics, Analyses ➤	➤ ROI Growth
Strategic Alliances ➤	➤ Networking
Research-Self ➤	➤ Research-Competitors
60 Seconds to Connect ➤	➤ Start with the End in Mind
Business Plan ➤	➤ Branding
Desire ➤	➤ Achievement

EMPLOYEE ENGAGEMENT: THE CONNECTION BEYOND SHOWING UP FOR WORK

"There are only three measurements that tell you nearly everything you need to know about your organization's overall performance: employee engagement, customer satisfaction, and cash flow…It goes without saying that no company, small or large, can win over the long run without energized employees who believe in the mission and understand how to achieve it…"

Jack Welch, former CEO of GE

CHAPTER 9

We can't talk about connection and not talk about Employee Engagement. It's been a "new" buzz term for a while, replacing the continuing conversation on "empowerment." Engaged employees present an entirely different level of confidence and connection both to co-

workers and to the customers they serve. When done correctly, this can take the roof off of what companies can achieve short term and long term as well.

According to the Corporate Leadership Council, employees with lower engagement levels are four times more likely to leave their jobs than those who are highly engaged. But the importance of employee engagement isn't just increased employee retention, it's also about higher productivity. One study by HR strategy firm Kenexa found that of 64 organizations studied, the organizations with highly engaged employees achieved twice the annual net income of organizations whose employees were less engaged.

Are your company's employees highly engaged? Let's talk about it through the eyes and written words of Elizabeth Veliz, owner of Adelante HR Consulting, L.L.C.

Webster Defines Employee Engagement very loosely. The definition centers around commitment; putting a ring on someone's finger; engaging in an activity.

Dozens of definitions exist for employee engagement, each one being different or exactly the same as the next. Wikipedia's definition is far more academic than any other I have seen:

> "Employee engagement is an emergent property of the relationship between an organization and its employees. An "engaged employee" is one who is fully absorbed by and enthusiastic about their work and so

takes positive action to further the organization's reputation and interests."

So, what does this mean in terms of desire and the full connection when it comes to people–your employees? I will offer my definition as part of the answer.

Defining **Employee Engagement** as:

1) *An emotional state of being* where employees come to work for a greater purpose than their paycheck and benefits.

Defining **Strategy** as:

1) A high-level plan to achieve one or more goals under conditions of uncertainty.

Defining **Purpose** as:

1) The reason for which something exists or is done, made, used, etc.
2) An intended or desired result; end; aim; goal.
3) Determination; resoluteness.
4) The subject at hand; the point at issue.
5) Practical result, effect or advantage: to act to good purpose.

Defining **Disconnected** as:

1) Having a connection broken.
2) As a person, lacking contact with reality.

Defining **Intentional Actions** as:

1) Design with a plan, with intent.
2) One with intention or on purpose; intended.

It is about creating that connection between the people who work in your organization and all of the parts and pieces of your organization–the mission, vision, values, goals, strategic plans, clients, suppliers, processes, etc. It is about creating a work environment that fuels desire in people–the *desire* to come to work on time, every day, ready to give 150% regardless of the obstacles and challenges that lie ahead. Superior performance and results can really only be achieved through intentional actions driven by desire. Rarely do we read about a "most admired" company that achieves superior results through coercion and force. Actually, I'm not certain I've ever read about such an organization anywhere.

The biggest challenge with tackling the employee engagement monster is proving to senior and executive leadership that there is value in investing time, resources and yes–oftentimes, money in this strategy. Let me stop here for a moment and focus on the word I just used–*strategy.* Employee engagement must be a *strategy* in your organization in order for the organization to reap its rewards. Any time employee engagement is a ***program, initiative or process it is destined to fail.*** All of these terms imply a beginning, middle and end. Here's a cliché if you've ever heard one: Employee engagement is a journey. I've heard this one before as well. Yes, it is a journey–but it is first and foremost a *strategy.*

Building a business case for employee engagement is not as easy as pulling the infinite amount of studies that show its impact on productivity, safety, quality, retention and operating margins; however, I would be remiss not to share a small sample of its potential impact on your organization. Here is a small taste of the power of employee engagement:

According to Gallup, organizations with a highly engaged workforce enjoy 22% higher productivity, 48% fewer safety incidents, 41% fewer patient safety incidents, and 41 % fewer quality incidents. According to Towers Watson, operating margins for organizations with highly engaged employees are 4-17% higher than in organizations with disengaged employees. Staggering numbers aren't they?

Employee engagement is not just for the big players, the Fortune 500 companies of the world. It is a universal sense of purpose applicable to all employees in all organizations from the minimum wage earners to the six- and seven-figure salaried professionals. The size of your paycheck does not determine your level of engagement.

Marcia and the Dress Connection

I remember walking into a Ross Department Store a few years ago looking for some summer clothing. I had lost a decent amount of weight and needed some newer, edgier attire. I pulled dozens of articles from the racks and made my way to the fitting room. I was greeted by an employee who appeared to be in her forties. As I tried on outfit after outfit, I realized I

was not happy with what I was seeing in the mirror. I decided to try on the final summer dress regardless of my discontent with my choices. As I stepped out of my fitting room and stood in front of the common area mirror, I uttered some self-deprecating phrases to the reflection. This particular employee, Marcia, responded to my insults with, "I don't know why you are saying that. You look absolutely beautiful in that dress. As a matter of fact, I went out and grabbed a few more for you while you were in the dressing room." In the true essence of making a long story short, Marcia had overheard my self-criticism the entire time I was in there. She took it upon herself to go find me clothing that she felt would look amazing on me. As I tried on everything she chose, she marveled at how great it all looked. I felt terrific and I spent a small fortune in the store as a result. Now, Marcia does not work on commission, nor was I the only person who had the privilege of this level of service from her. I overheard her managing other fitting room dilemmas with the same level of service, compassion and yes, purpose. She was fully connected. I imagine that Marcia does not make a six- or seven-figure income, but somehow she was fully connected–engaged. I spoke to the manager of the store and expressed my sincere gratitude for the gem of a salesperson she had in Marcia. The manager looked incredibly proud as she told me that Marcia was always getting compliments from customers and that she would be sure to pass my praise along to her in the next staff meeting. That just made my day.

Check Point

1) Can you list names from your staff, employees who show these exact signs of being fully engaged and who understand their purpose within the company?

____

____

____

2) If not, why not? Dig deep and figure out why you can't name names. If so, when's the last time you told them "thank you" and truly showed appreciation and gave recognition in a way that personally and continually motivates them?

____

____

____

3) Make a list of ideas if you haven't yet thanked them in a very authentic and purposeful way.

____

____

____

The Disconnected CEO

From a different perspective, let me offer you the story of the disconnected CEO. I was consulting for a small business owner who was looking to either grow the organization and retire, or sell it completely. I didn't think it was possible to have

someone at the head of a very successful, multi-million dollar enterprise be "actively" disengaged. Yes, the CEO was actually causing chaos and damage inside of his own organization. He was so disenchanted with the business–as successful as it was–that he was making sure he would spread misery to all he was in contact with. He was known for delivering bad news on a Friday afternoon and telling the recipients, "Good, now your weekend is ruined too." He was known for playing favorites, for ignoring the expert guidance and counsel of HR and for making obviously detrimental business decisions. The employees themselves confessed that the CEO was "checked out…disconnected."

Check Point

1) Do your actions reflect connection or disconnection? What examples can you think of immediately to confirm your thoughts and perspective?

    ____

    ____

    ____

CONNECTION THROUGH INTENTIONAL ACTIONS

It is clear that regardless of rank, salary, power position or role, anyone is susceptible to becoming disconnected. Employee engagement is not achieved by accident or circumstance. It is the result of intentional actions by leaders in an organization. It takes commitment, patience, purpose and a focused effort. Employee engagement is so much more than just having great leadership development and recognition programs in place. It is about focusing on every aspect of the business that touches, influences or impacts employee engagement. It is far more complex than what the traditional approach to employee engagement has been. It is about examining every part of your business and looking at employee engagement holistically in order to create the fully connected workforce.

Here's a list of how you can connect with a holistic approach to Employee Engagement designed by Elizabeth Veliz from her book *Employee Engagement: The Holistic Approach to A Fully Connected Workforce.*

Vision and Mission

Values

Talent Acqusition

Onboarding

KPIs/Goals/Objectives

Performance Management

Total Rewards

Recognition

Employee Development

Career Ascension/Career Enhancement

Leadership Development

Culture

ACTION IS CALLING: Employee Engagement Checkup Questions.

Whether you are getting started or are already in the midst of this journey, the following are just a few of the questions you should be asking about your organization:

1) Are our employees engaged like Marcia? Why or why not?

   ____

   ____

2) How are we measuring employee engagement?

   ____

   ____

3) Are we committed to employee engagement or are we simply content with "programs?"

   ____

   ____

4) What aspects of our business impact employee engagement and how are we doing in each of those areas?

   ____

   ____

5) Why do I or should I care about my/our employee engagement?

   ____

   ____

6) What benchmark are we using? How often are we taking an internal pulse?

____

____

7) What does or will our culture allow? Do our mission and vision allow employee engagement to begin now or in the future?

____

____

____

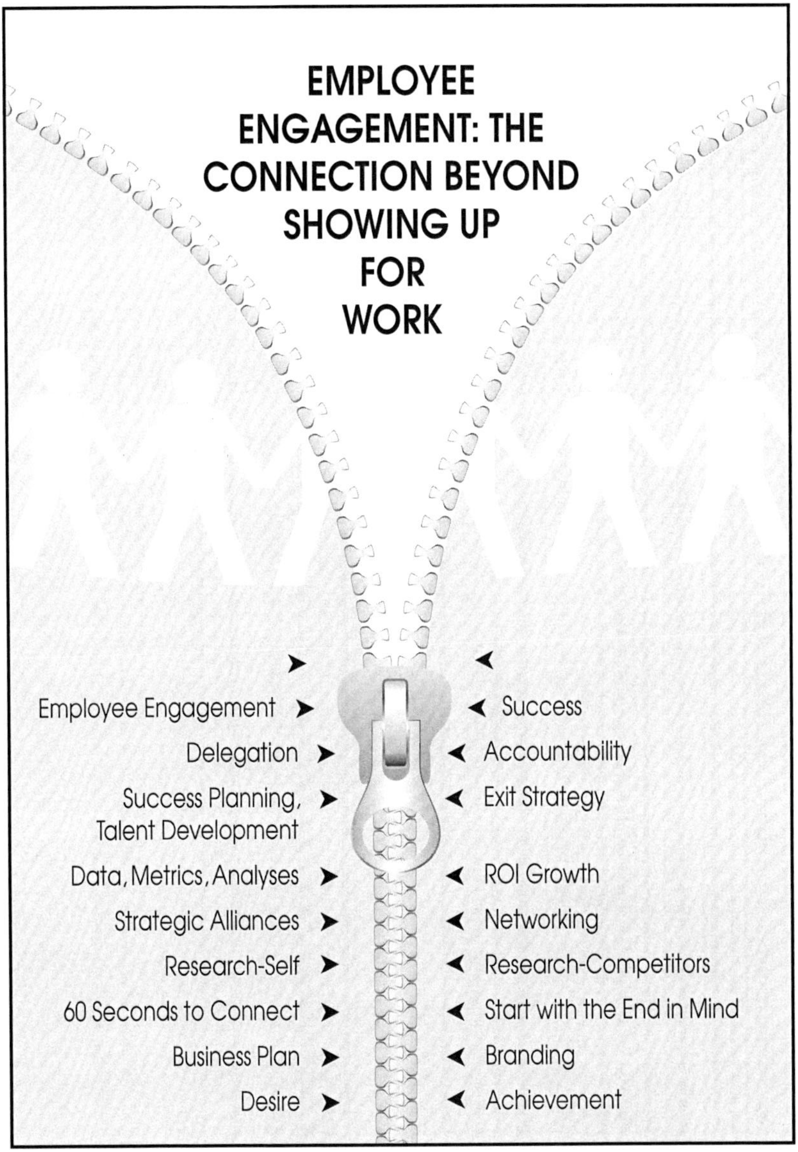

EMPLOYEE ENGAGEMENT: THE CONNECTION BEYOND SHOWING UP FOR WORK

Employee Engagement ➤	◀ Success
Delegation ➤	◀ Accountability
Success Planning, Talent Development ➤	◀ Exit Strategy
Data, Metrics, Analyses ➤	◀ ROI Growth
Strategic Alliances ➤	◀ Networking
Research-Self ➤	◀ Research-Competitors
60 Seconds to Connect ➤	◀ Start with the End in Mind
Business Plan ➤	◀ Branding
Desire ➤	◀ Achievement

WAVE OF CONNECTIVITY: FINAL THOUGHTS

"I define connection as the energy that exists between people when they feel seen, heard, and valued; when they can give and receive without judgment; and when they derive sustenance and strength from the relationship."

Brené Brown

CHAPTER 10

There are lots of excuses one can make to oneself for not being great. It's easier not to take risks than it is to take risks because of fear; fear about money, taxes, loneliness, insecurity, your mortgage, unemployment and, of course, nay-saying people. Any of these can scare you away from operating independently or imaginatively. Greatness through connection is, in my opinion, the uprooting of such fears. Why? Because on the other side of fear is success and the wave of connectivity in business and life.

When we place barriers and allow others to place them we impede our progress. When you see through the barriers to the other side, then and only then can you connect to

something entirely new. You allow yourself and those connected to you to become free. You open your mind to possibilities, and disruption is no longer an option.

I believe that each of us, in our way and in our own worlds, can effect positive change by embracing the kind of connecting spirit outlined and suggested in this book. When we choose to connect and embrace all of the opportunities out there, there will be a significant impact on how we do business in the future.

To enjoy the waves of your own connectivity, you have to be open, think openly, decide what is important and make it happen. Welcome new approaches and ideas. Don't be afraid to ask for help and seek out all the connecting opportunities right in front of you every day. Don't be afraid to connect with others to make your world a better place.

Defining **Wave** as:

1) A back-and-forth motion around a reference value.
2) A kind of oscillation (disturbance) that travels through space and matter.
3) Wave motions transfer energy from one place to another.

Defining **Connectivity** as:

1) To join with or become joined to something else.
2) To think of (something or someone) as being related to or involved with.

Define **Embracing** as:

1) To embrace something is to welcome it with open arms.
2) To accept something completely.

We cultivate our connections when we allow our most vulnerable and powerful selves to be deeply seen and known, and when we honor the connection that grows from that offering with trust, respect, kindness and affection. Connecting is not something we give or get; it is something that we nurture and grow, a connection that can only be cultivated between two or more people and businesses when it exists within each one of them. We can only expect to connect with others if we first understand our part and role in the wave of connectivity itself and see the power of change that can occur when the ultimate connection is made.

CONNECTION OPPORTUNITY REMINDER

We may never know what opportunities we may have missed in life by showing up tightfisted. It's hard to receive anything if we don't open our hands to give. This is as true in our personal lives as it is in business. Take the example of a travel agency. You book a cruise with one agency and you get good service, but nothing else. Another travel agency also provides good service, but goes the extra step of having a bottle of wine greet you in your cabin, along with a personalized note. Sometimes the difference between keeping

and losing a customer in a competitive market is nothing more than the cost of a $30 bottle of wine.

Check Point

1) When's the last time you went the extra mile? Do you have a piece of business coming up soon that gives you an opportunity to be remembered by the customer?

____

____

____

____

THE REFERRAL CONNECTION

Let's talk about our connections that give referrals to us: "No referral should be left behind." Referrals that translate into a business deal not only generate revenue, they also save you time and money in your sales expenses and sales cycle. For a small business, in particular, they are golden currency. It's surprising how many individuals don't reciprocate beyond saying thank you in an email that requires less effort and energy than the person expended in providing the referral. A handwritten note to let the person know how much you appreciate the referral is a more caring way of responding. Add a small gift certificate to Starbucks, some theater tickets or a box of chocolates—any token of your appreciation. If the business deal was substantial, make it more personal with an invitation to dinner to genuinely show your gratitude. It's the old-school way of doing business. It's being human.

Check Point

1) What have you done for your referring connections? Stop and think now, make a list and get right to it if you're behind. It's never too late. Better late than never is very relevant here.

____

____

____

____

____

CONNECTING THROUGH QUALITY CONTENT

Don't tease people by providing some small content and monetizing the rest. Freely share quality content, on a regular basis, to engender good will and develop a following. It will come back to you in different ways. Ask your followers online what information would be most helpful to them. Research problems your customers might be having in their businesses and publish answers on your blog, your video blog, so they can see and hear your passion. Or better yet via Google Hangout. Using Google Hangout, you can invite them to join in live, a fantastic way to connect instantly.

Check Point

1) What type of content do you provide on your website, blog or newsletters?

2) What opportunities do you have to better connect to your followers?
3) If you were being interviewed, what would your potential connectors want to know about your business? How could they benefit from your answers? Make a bullet point list of your top ten items. You aren't giving away "secrets," you are gaining respect for your knowledge, building credibility and confidence to share with and help others.
    a. ____________________________
    b. ____________________________
    c. ____________________________
    d. ____________________________
    e. ____________________________
    f. ____________________________
    g. ____________________________
    h. ____________________________
    i. ____________________________
    j. ____________________________

CONNECTING WITHOUT EXPECTATIONS

The basic principle of connecting is to give without any expectation. A common Chinese proverb says, "Forget the favors you have given; remember those received." When we do favors, or go the extra mile with the intention of collecting later, something inevitably leaks through in our interaction with others. People can smell this a mile away. Making people feel obligated through your "connection" backfires, as they resent it. It also diminishes the initial act. Finally, as we discuss giving, give to those who can be of no use to you. John Wooden put it beautifully: "You can't live a perfect day without doing something for someone who will never be able to repay you."

LISTEN AND YOU WILL CONNECT

Editorial cartoonist Frank Tyger once said, "There is no greater loan than a sympathetic ear." In today's noisy world, filled with distractions, people are starved for someone who truly listens. Listening is one of the kindest connecting activities. Give your employees and colleagues the gift of your attention by carving out time to listen to their problems, hopes and aspirations.

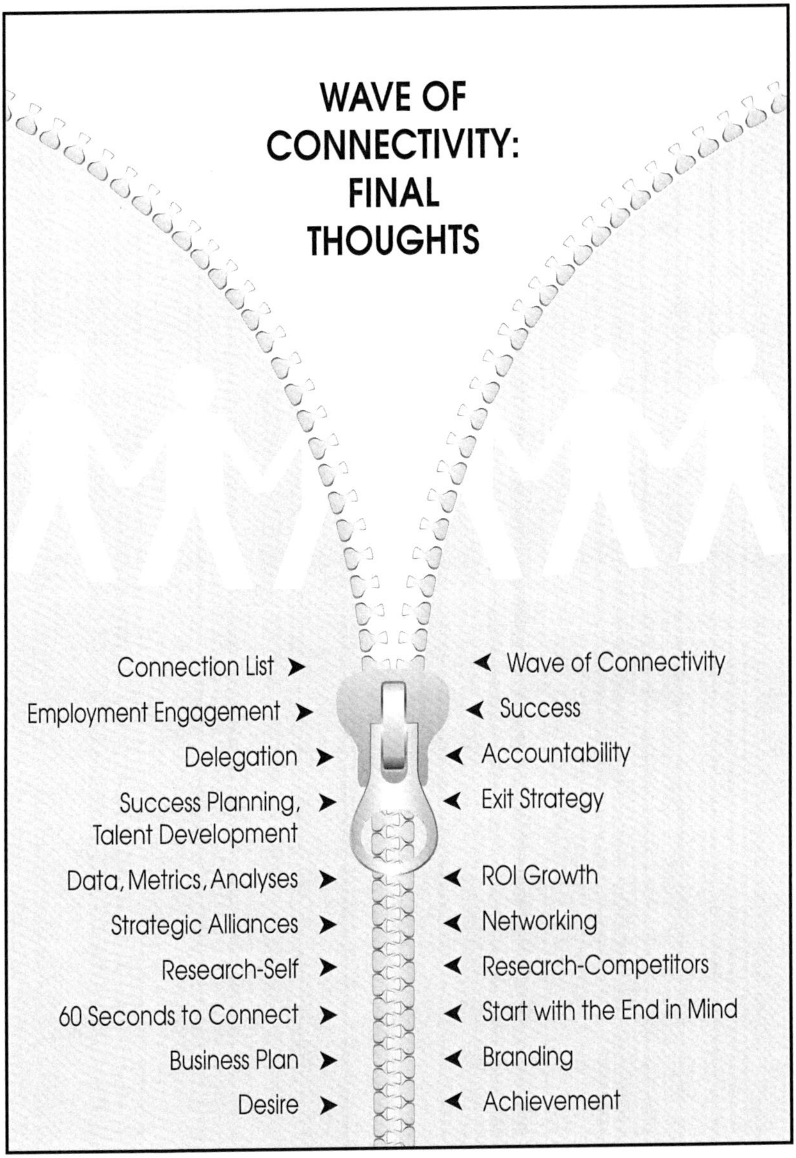

WAVE OF CONNECTIVITY: FINAL THOUGHTS

Connection List ➤	◀ Wave of Connectivity
Employment Engagement ➤	◀ Success
Delegation ➤	◀ Accountability
Success Planning, Talent Development ➤	◀ Exit Strategy
Data, Metrics, Analyses ➤	◀ ROI Growth
Strategic Alliances ➤	◀ Networking
Research-Self ➤	◀ Research-Competitors
60 Seconds to Connect ➤	◀ Start with the End in Mind
Business Plan ➤	◀ Branding
Desire ➤	◀ Achievement

THE LIST OF CONNECTIONS: One Last Checkup

This is not meant to be all inclusive but certainly a beginning. How does your list look? How many of these connections are your connections, too?

- ✓ Connecting your Desires and Passions in life to your "average" day's events.
- ✓ Connecting and sharing your natural Talents with your hardwired Behaviors to your life's story.
- ✓ Connecting your business no matter how big or small to
    - Your Vision
    - Your Mission
    - The Culture
    - Key Competencies
    - Matching Behaviors
    - Key Performance Indicators
- ✓ Connecting the Data to the Metrics to the Plan to the Action
- ✓ Connecting the Right People to the Right Projects
- ✓ Connecting Words to Action
- ✓ Connecting the Ability to Review and Pivot

- ✓ Connecting your Resources and the Ability to use them all
- ✓ Connecting the Need and Ability to ask for help– you can't do it all and you aren't supposed to go through life and business alone
- ✓ Connecting to the Right Networking groups for your business, your trade, your soul
- ✓ Connecting Spiritually
- ✓ Connecting and having life's Balance and overall Wellness
- ✓ Connecting to the RIGHT strategic partners, even those you used to perceive as competitors
- ✓ Connecting and utilizing your own Strengths
- ✓ Connecting to others that make your Weaknesses go away
- ✓ Connecting and seizing the day on the right Opportunities
- ✓ Connecting and asking for help to mitigate the Threats around you
- ✓ Connecting your colleagues to their own personal Training and Development
- ✓ Connecting through proper Communication
- ✓ Connecting to Others, whether a mentor, friend, colleague and or leader
- ✓ Connecting Leadership to the awesome responsibility of helping people and companies grow
- ✓ Connecting your ideas as an Entrepreneur with those who can make your idea come alive and prosper

- ✓ Connecting Others to work that is outside of your scope
- ✓ Connecting and staying Focused to what you do best
- ✓ Connecting your Revenue Streams to your biggest Return on Investments
- ✓ Connecting and placing the Right People with the Right Jobs in your business and organization
- ✓ Connecting others to the knowledge and sharing of your Experiences and Lessons Learned
- ✓ Connecting your 60-Second Introduction to
    - Who you are
    - What you offer
    - How you do what you do
    - WHY you do what you do
- ✓ Connecting your Fears to your Opportunities and Possibilities

THE CONNECTION
Book Collection List

BOOK TITLE	AUTHOR(S)	FOCUS
Touching History: The Untold Story of the Drama That Unfolded in the Skies Over America	Lynn Spencer	Bravery, Leadership and Your Average Day
Blue Ocean Strategy - How to Create Uncontested Market Space and Make the Competition Irrelevant	W. Chan Kim & Renee Mauborgne	Marketing, Business Plan
Book Yourself Solid	Michael Port & Jocelyn Wallace	Marketing, Branding, Business Development
Business Model Generation & Business Model You	Alexander Ostewalder & Yves Pigneur	Everything Business, Road Map, Entreprenuerial, Freelancing
Change Anything - The New Science of Personal Success	Kerry Patterson, Joseph Grenny, David Maxfield, Ron McMillian, and Al Switzler	Motivational

Fit to Lead	Christoper P. Neck,PH.D., Tedd L. Mitchell, M.D., Charles C. Manz, PH.D., Emmet C. Thompson II, D.S.L.	Motivational, Health, Leadership, Responsibility
Founding Sisters and the Nineteenth Amendment	Eleanor Clift	Strength, Motivation
Hardwiring Excellence	Quint Studer	Motivational
How to Deliver A Ted Talk	Jeremey Donovan	Business, Leadership, Focus
Just as You Are	Paul Coutinho, SJ	Motivational
Light Bulbs For Leaders/ A Guide Book For Team Learning	Barbara Pate Glacel & Emile A. Robert, Jr.	Leadership, Collaboration
Made To Stick	Chip & Dan Heath	Business Longevity
Midnight Lunch	Sarah Miller Caldicott	Collaboration, Motivation, Leadership

Multipliers - How the Best Leaders Make Everyone Smarter	Liz Wiseman	Leadership, Responsibility, Self-Awareness
Reality Is Broken	Jane Mcgonigal	Motivational
Stop Organizing Start Producing	Casey Moore	Productivity at the Highest Level
The Education of a Coach	David Halberstam	Motivational
The Fifth Discipline	Peter M. Senge	Leadership, Collaboration, Focus, Production
The Lean Startup	Eric Ries	Entrepreneurship
The Startup Owner's Manual	Steve Blank & Bob Dorf	Entrepreneurship
Those We Love Most	Lee Woodruff	Motivational
Time Power	Charles R. Hobbs	Motivational, Inspirational, Self-Awareness

To Sell Is Human	Daniel H. Pink	Excellence, Self-Awareness, Business Development
Leadership Conversations: Challenging High Potential Managers to Become Great Leaders	Alan S. Bernson and Richard G. Stieglitz	Leadership, Collaboration, Development
Give and Take: Why Helping Others Drives Our Success	Adam M. Grant	Community, Collaboration

NOTES

NOTES